My RV Mentor

My RV Mentor

For the Newbie and the Experienced

Jack Hunnicutt

Acknowledgement

To my Followers, Subscribers and Viewers who unknowingly contributed to and inspired my creative efforts in writing this book.

Table of Contents

ix

Foreword

Learning is a never-ending journey in which we are all guilty, on a daily if not hourly basis. Travel and learning are so closely related you can't have one without the other even if the travel is only to the front porch to pick up the morning newspaper.

My Book and my associated blog and YouTube channel are more about the journey than the destination. There, I choose to focus on the oh so complicated technology and machinery making the journey possible. My hopes for this book are for you to avoid the so-called "school of hard knocks" and make the transition to RV Owner as quickly and smoothly as possible. And I truly think you can.

When I began my RV adventures many years ago, I relied on friends and fellow RV owners to steer me in the right direction and with that along with a big dose of trial and error I learned how to operate my RV and to navigate the complex details of traveling with your "home" attached to the back of your vehicle. The learning piece of RV ownership is a never-ending journey.

There are shortcuts to most anything and especially with recreational vehicles, the shortcuts often, will cost you in the long run. I do strongly believe there is a better mouse trap out there somewhere, but I also believe that speeding kills, shoddy maintenance will catch up with you and camping is fun, period. Begin with the basics and improve as you go is a good approach to staying safe while enjoying your new experiences and making friends along the way.

My RV Mentor is a work of love allowing me to leverage my past experiences learning the ropes, taking the good with the bad and all the great memories along the way. And yes, I have made mistakes and wasted money along the way but keep in mind that with mistakes valuable lessons are learned and your knowledge expands. By sharing my recommendations, suggestions and experiences I hope to help and inspire you to realize your potential and rise to the challenge at hand.

I learned a valuable lesson in RV driving school many years ago which is not to worry about what people are thinking about you as you go down the road because in all likelihood, they will never see you again. But we need to be responsible for our actions to one another, to the environment and to the RVing community at large. Do what is right, do what is safe, respect others and leave the public with a feeling the RV community is something to be respected if not envied.

I strongly encourage you to use the resources identified in this book and to reach out to others and even to me, as necessary. Interacting with fellow RV Owners on the My RV Mentor Facebook Group is a great way to continuedly expand your knowledge and before long you will be Mentoring others.

Confidence is your friend, yet fear keeps everything in check.

Jack Hunnicutt
December 2020

How to Use this Book

This is a reference book for both quick reference and in-depth study of specific subject matter. You may read these chapters in any order that fulfills your needs or desires. Although much the material is interrelated each chapter is an independent study of a system, concept, method or a particular activity such as buying, driving or planning.

With a high emphasis on learning and developing the skills of a new RV Owner or as a refreshed to the experienced, each chapter has space for taking notes, making diagrams or recording questions for future research. You may also want to use this space to record the specifics of your RV such as size and number of holding tanks, number and type of batteries, location of the converter and inverter, tire size and tire pressure and the actual height or your RV for bridge and tunnel clearance purposes.

The book is divided into seven Parts, grouping chapters together that are closely related. The following short descriptions of each Part is provided for quick reference and may help in choosing chapters and reading priority.

Part I - Begins with developing your RV purchasing process and how a specific RV selection would fit your desired lifestyle or recreational needs. Here we explore the myths surrounding recreational vehicles and take a look at each of the different types of recreational vehicles attempting to answer the question "which is the best match for my family?" We walk through the buying process with tips on discounts, considerations for local verses out of town dealers and the importance of establishing a good service relationship. Descriptions of RV weights and towing capacities are discussed. I remove the mystery behind the pre-delivery inspection and simplify the process ensuring you drive away with an RV fully functioning and ready to go camping. Rounding out the new purchase experience is setting the stage for the first night's camping and how to maximize the learning experience while camping and enjoying your RV.

Part II - Takes the new owner into the campground covering techniques for driving and backing the RV. Inside tips on backing trailers and how they differ from motorhomes. Then transitions to the unhitching and setup of the RV as we settle in at the campsite.

Part III - Addresses the major RV systems and components. Starting with the holding tanks and freshwater management, we will learn the purpose of each holding tank and how to maintain and use the tanks. We learn tips on how to avoid freshwater cross-contamination and how to store the various hoses, filters, and fittings. The electrical system is broken down into 12 volt and 110 volt systems for ease of understanding and troubleshooting. Appliances are discussed in terms of how each is powered on either by electricity or liquid propane (LP) and common troubleshooting steps. And finally, tires and batteries are discussed from the perspective of safety and cost savings. You will learn how to inspect tires and how to maintain proper air pressure while also learning how to maintain the batteries and how to prevent premature battery failure.

Part IV - Discusses how to deal with roadside emergencies and provides tips on how to take proactive steps in securing your RV and protecting it from theft. Safety considerations are discussed, and safety devices are identified and described.

Part V - Identifies the planning tools and methods for trip planning, making reservations and obtaining camping discounts. We also discuss National and State Parks and various discount programs. Common clubs, discounts memberships, and subscriptions are described noting advantages of each and associated costs. Tips and safety concerns are outlined, and a checklist is provided to minimize driving distractions while establishing a driving routine. Alternative camping opportunities are described for free camping with minimal or no facilities provided.

Part VI - Is a mixture of several subjects including caring for your RV while not in use and specifics on storage concerns. Campground etiquette expectations are provided to ensure the New Owner feels at home in the campground and understands how to be a good neighbor. For equipping the new RV, a list of the top 10 must have items is provided and tips on making purchases to save time and money. Understanding solar power and generators; how they supplement the Airstream's power needs and choosing appropriate system configurations to enhance your boondocking and dry camping experiences.

Part VII - In this section we bring it all together, first taking consideration for the pets that tag along on our travels. Then a look at RV quality and managing expectations on maintenance and repairs. And finally, some closing guidance on the journey from RV Newbie to RV Pro. Here the author gives the reader a challenge on sharing their new knowledge and completing a set of RV and camping activities to demonstrate the skill and knowledge they have obtained from this book.

The Appendices add a significant level of detail to the book and provides a quick reference on troubleshooting, common questions, recommended tools, online resources, and a description of RV Jargon.

Part I

Everyone wants to live on top of the mountain, but all the happiness and growth occurs while you're climbing it.

~Andy Rooney

Grand Tetons - Near Jackson Hole, Wyoming

Making the Decision

It's not every day you make a lifestyle change but believe it or not becoming a recreational vehicle (RV) owner is a change that will affect your leisure time, finances and in some way family relationships. In other words, it's not a decision to take lightly without significant planning and research. And therefore you have my book and why I am happy to show you how you can do everything involving your RV with confidence.

In this book I will assume you are motivated or at least highly interested in making the plunge into RV ownership but are not sure what steps to take first, or how to prevent getting in over your head. Additionally, you are concerned about matching your family to the perfect RV while at the same time worried that your needs may be changing over time as the family evolves. These are all valid concerns since the adventure you are about to undertake is exciting, challenging, and invigorating while at the same time being mostly downright scary. I and every other RV owner has been in your shoes and completely understand what it means to be a Newbie. Set aside your worries and remember that every other RV owner has survived the challenge and you will too.

So first I will lay out the obvious constraints you are facing as an RV owner:
- For the average family, it can and probably will be expensive.
- Vacations will and should involve the RV (you want to get your money's worth, right?)
- Upkeep and maintenance will not take care of itself; ongoing responsibility/expense.
- Parking/storage is necessary when not in use. Neighborhood and Homeowner's Association rules apply.
- Vehicle registration and insurance every year.
- Steep uphill learning curve since all of this is new.

That steep learning curve is exactly what we are going to resolve for you in this book. Your learning time will be reduced, you will maximize your RV knowledge quickly and together we will put that Newbie status in the rear-view mirror. Using what I give you here and some hands-on experience, you will transition from "RV Newbie to Pro" very quickly. It really depends on how often you camp and how many days you spend on the road.

What always comes up first is "What style, class, brand or make of RV do I want or need?" There are an unlimited number of answers to this question and the advice I have is to approach it like buying a pair of shoes; go and try some on to see if they fit. RV dealers want you to look at and consider their products and they will offer advice and suggestions but remember one thing, they are in the business of selling what is on their lot and not necessarily getting you into that perfect RV.

You will want to visit several dealers to ensure you see a good cross section of brands and styles or better yet go to an RV show. Usually in the winter and spring manufactures and/or dealers will gather a large selection of RVs in one location for your viewing and buying pleasure. Using the Internet, web forums or Facebook groups is a good place to ask about scheduled shows.

Shop like you're buying a house, furniture, and car all at the same time. Imagine you family relaxing, eating, and sleeping in each style and floorplan you view. Lay on the bed, sit in the chairs, even step in the shower and toilet and size it up to make sure it fits your body. Think carefully about how you will store you clothing, shoes, and cosmetics. Additionally, think about the kitchen items like food, dishes, and cleaning products. Don't forget about the pets and their needs like food, water bowls and their bed.

The big differences between Fifth Wheels, Travel Trailers and Motorhomes are primarily how you prefer to travel going down the road because they all sleep, cook, shower and eat about the same. The two trailers, fifth wheels and travel trailers, require a tow vehicle sufficient for towing and it possibly could be used as your daily driving vehicle when not camping. Plan and ensure you have a sufficient and safe match between tow vehicle and trailer. All too often someone buys a trailer then realizes their tow vehicle is not up to the challenge. I recommend thoroughly resolving all these weight calculations and towing capacities before making commitments on a specific RV and in the long run it will save you money and valuable time.

Motorhomes (Class A, B and C) on the other hand are an all-in-one unit nicely packaged in a self-contained vehicle virtually ready to hit the road. Maintaining the motorhome requires much more effort and frequently more expense than a trailer. This is directly related to the motorhome sitting unused for long periods of time which takes a toll on the motorhome's chassis and drivetrain.

In the big picture of RV choices there are pros and cons to all configurations (which is covered in the next chapter) but as I stated, it usually comes down to *how you want to travel and not how you want to camp.* I have owned all three and my major considerations are:

- Motorhomes sit unused for long periods of time which isn't good for mechanical systems.
- Fifth Wheel slide outs usually prevent entrance into the unit with the slides retracted, and they can be very high with several steps.
- Travel Trailers to some drivers are more difficult to tow and park, require weight distribution and anti-sway hitches.

Pro Tip: Don't rush through the decision-making process and never force the round peg into the square hole. Most decisions are reversible only if you are willing to live with the cost. And never assume full-time RV life is cheap. It may be less expensive than a brick-and-mortar home but daily camping fees, fuel, insurance and finally, routine, and unexpected maintenance adds up quickly.

Notable exceptions to these RV generalizations are the Truck Camper and Tiny Trailers. Both of these are for the minimalist who are highly mobile and often find their travels taking them off the beaten path.

The forerunner of all recreational vehicles, the truck camper has taken families camping for the pass 100 years. They began as a homemade contraption made to fit on a work truck for weekend adventures then removable freeing up the truck's bed for other purposes. This can be the cheapest entry point into RV ownership but don't exclude this as a viable option until you have seen what is available. Some truck campers can be relatively large and require a very robust truck to accommodate the size and weight while the smaller units can easily be carried on any typical half ton pickup.

Tiny Trailers are becoming popular especially for the tent campers who want to expand their camping experience without limiting camping locations. The small size has many advantages if you are willing to live with the constraints.

Enough room to sleep two adults with an outside galley is what keeps these trailers small, light and compact. They can be towed by the average passenger vehicle which can be a significant cost saver to get started. Some even have a small air conditioner while others only have 12 volt DC power available. The options and functionality varies so greatly requiring the potential buyer to be very savvy on what the trailer can offer and what their specific camping style demands.

If you feel I'm over thinking this whole decision-making process well I probably am. It sounds much more complex and over whelming that it really is because much of what I have described will come naturally and will be almost intuitive as you step through your decision-making process.

At this point you have begun to collect resources to guide you down the path and help to keep it all manageable. You may be surprised at what value family, friends and work associates can bring to the table if you simply ask. Finding a camping buddy who has experience could be the ingredient to making this cake bake right and taste good.

Starting with this chapter I incorporate some blank space to take notes, record questions and itemize your particular needs. I encourage you to write in this book and refer to the information as you go forward on this journey.

Notes:

RV Myths

Anyone that has spent one night in an RV will remember that experience for the rest of their lives. Unfortunately, when someone makes an authoritative statement about RVs or most anything, we tend to take it as truth and accurate and remember that for the rest of our lives as well. But this isn't always the case. We just sometimes believe exactly what we hear because we have no experience in that arena and we follow along like little well-behaved sheep; thus, myths are born. Baaaah…

There are many so-called myths about things like, which manufacturer is best, who has the best quality, which are four-season camping ready and on and on. These are issues founded on opinion or choice and don't really have a correct answer. Whereas the following are "assumed facts" that have no foundation in truth and can become very misleading.

1. Recreational vehicles are hard to drive or tow. It may seem so at first if you have never operated a commercial size vehicle. For some it may even be intimidating. But just like the first time you drove years ago, everything new and unknown may seem overwhelming at first. Once you overcome the newness, it's just a learning process. Learn to compensate for wide turns, always be aware of your vehicle height and just slow down. Experience will build confidence and sooner than you think, the "white-knuckle" driving will go away.

2. RV travel saves money on hotels. Using a very elementary comparison; staying 294 nights in a hotel at $85/night would pay for a $25,000 RV. Hotel living would certainly be cheaper over the long run if you are willing to give up experiencing living close to nature and enjoying outside activities like cooking, hiking and stargazing. I think most of us value sleeping in our own bed with our special pillow, and not worrying about who slept here last.

3. RVs requires a Special Driver's License. The quick answer is no. A Special Driver's License is not required "except" in very specific cases. The general guideline is not to exceed 26,000 lb. or 45 feet (40 in CA) in length. A quick Internet search will provide the specifics for each state.

4. Recreational vehicles must stop at state operated weigh stations. The weigh stations you see located along the Interstate Highway System and other roadways, are for commercial vehicles only. If your vehicle or trailer is for personal use you are not considered commercial, however once you put a sign on you rig (Avon, Mary Kay, Joe's Window Tinting) your vehicle may be considered commercial.

5. Living in an RV is just like living at home, but smaller. This is a huge concern for families with children or people considering full-time camping. Yes, the RV is smaller, and it gets even smaller the longer you are in it. Add in a couple of children and a pet or two and it's like living in a submarine with windows. Complete privacy is nonexistent except for a short bathroom visit. It takes readjustment for everyone and after a couple of trips (3 or 4 at most) you will have a system worked out on how to manage space "and people." When shopping for an RV ensure you bring the entire family along to see how they fit in the prospective RV models.

6. Campgrounds don't allow older RVs. For some unjustified reason this is a concern that some people worry about. There are a very few "resort type" campgrounds that have a 10 year or similar cutoff requirement for recreational vehicles. In my 20 years+ RV traveling and camping, I have yet to run across this limitation. But I do know those campgrounds do exist, however they are rare exceptions. If you find yourself at one of these campgrounds, ask for an inspection to see if your RV is acceptable and if it is not, you are probably better off going somewhere else where everyone is camping on equal terms.

7. Walmart always offers Free Camping. Not true. Some offer overnight Free Parking based upon local policy and ordinances. Some prohibit all overnight parking. It is always best to call ahead and ask if overnight parking is authorized. Just remember, you are parking and not camping so don't bring out the awning, camp chairs, grills and limit the use of slides. If you must put out a slide to access the bedroom that is fine, just be aware of traffic flow around your RV.

8. Any Roadside Service is good enough for my RV. Many roadside service plans do not cover recreational vehicles such as, auto insurance plans and even standard AAA plans. Motorhomes and RV trailers require special equipment for towing and tire service. When shopping for roadside service inquire about coverage for your specific RV (weight and length) to ensure you are not left stranded on the side of the road because of service refusal.

9. RV salespersons are experts in RV towing and hitches. When asked, "can my truck pull that RV?" the salesperson will typically say, "it can tow anything on the lot." Don't be fooled by this inaccurate and unsafe attitude. Configuring a towing solution for a trailer (5th wheel or travel trailer) or just towing an auto behind a motorhome, can be a complex process. Each vehicle has very specific weight and towing capacities determined by the manufacturer. Taking any antidotal advice from a salesperson, or anyone else, can lead to trouble or at a minimum, additional expense paying for a correct system after you learn you followed some bad advice. Seek a professional or do your own research and make intelligent decisions always with safety in mind.

10. Professional RV inspections are too expensive and not necessary. For most people when purchasing a new RV, a professional inspector is not necessary. This is because you have a warranty and when you conduct the dealer pre-delivery inspection (PDI) you will require the RV dealer to operate "everything" and demonstrate how to operate "everything." It

is a completely different story when buying a pre-owned unit. Most of us are not experts in determining the condition of the RV structure and operations of the many RV systems and components. Typically, an inspection will run $300 to $600 which is well worth the expense to know that everything is operational, there is no water damage, and you are provided a detailed listing of everything that is not operating as intended. I see too many cases of RV buyers finding out after the purchase that the unit has water damage, and the repair runs into the thousands of dollars.

11. You cannot flush toilet paper in an RV. This is a recreational vehicle myth of unknown origin but seems to have taken root especially with some newer RV owners. The real facts are that the toilet and holding tank are designed to handle "all" human waste. Later in the book you will learn the proper procedures to finally put this myth to rest. So no, you do not have to run to the bathhouse at 3 a.m. to take care of "emergency business."

12. And finally, it is okay to let a friend borrow my RV. We all like to share and help others to experience the joy of RV camping. But an RV is personal, complex and easily damaged. You are reading *My RV Mentor* because you want to learn about RVs, and you will quickly learn it is not something to take lightly. No one will respect and understand your RV like you can and this goes for family members as well. If someone asks, just let them know how much you had to study and learn before you were "good to go" and how much it cost for RV repairs. Running the batteries down to "dead" can cost several hundred dollars and it happens very easily to someone not familiar with managing RV power. Good luck with this one.

The origin of these myths probably involved some stereotyping and a few servings of adult beverages. People will believe what they will and there is little we can offer to change their minds except to be good examples. When it comes to recreational vehicles, or just about anything else, if we throw out all the exceptional good and all the exceptional bad, the actual myth busting truth is hiding right next to common sense.

RV Classes and Types

Keeping track of the different classes and types of recreational vehicles takes some time to learn. These comparisons may help to narrow down your options.

Motorhome

Class A

Pros	Cons
All in One Package	Expense
Bathroom available when Traveling	Drivetrain Sits Unused for Long Periods
Move Around Inside While Traveling	Tow Behind Vehicle May be Necessary
Use of Kitchen/Bath with Slides Extended	Upkeep Expense
Onboard Generator Capability	No Spare Tire
Basement Storage	

Class B

Pros	Cons
All in one package	Expense
Bathroom available when Traveling (Some Models)	Drivetrain Sits Unused for Long Periods
Move Around Inside While Traveling	Tow Behind Vehicle May be Necessary
Easy to Park in Typical Parking Lots	Small Living Space
No Special Driving Considerations	Limited Storage

Class C

Pros	Cons
All in One Package	Drivetrain Sits Unused for Long Periods
Bathroom available when Traveling	Tow Behind Vehicle May be Necessary
Move Around Inside While Traveling	Limited Cargo Carrying Capacity
Sleeping Space Over Cab (Most Models)	

Fifth Wheel

Pros	Cons
Most Inside Space of All Types	Limited Inside Access with Slides Retracted
Basement for Storage	Can be 13' 6" High
Onboard Generator Capability (Some Models)	Sits High Off the Ground
Most Models have Bathroom Access with Slides Retracted	Requires Pickup Truck with Hitch in Bed

Travel Trailer

Pros	Cons
Sits Low to the Ground	Limited Inside Access with Slides Retracted
Can be Towed with SUV or Half Ton Pickup (Some Models)	Limited Storage
Most Models have Bathroom Access with Slides Retracted	Propane Tanks Exposed on Front (Most Models)
Lowest Bridge/Tunnel Clearance of all Types	

Truck Camper

Pros	Cons
Can Go and Park Anywhere	Small Limited Space & Sleeping Capacity
Can Be Removed from Truck When Not in Use	No Full Bathroom
Least Expensive of All Types	
Some Access While Traveling	

Toy Hauler

The most versatile of all recreational vehicles, the Toy Hauler, really is a breed of its own. What makes these so unique is the rear multi-function compartment accessible by a ramp. The compartment is configured with tie down points to secure golf carts, 4-wheelers, motorcycles or a side by side. The ramp allows for easy rear access and some can be converted into a patio type platform for leisure enjoyment.

As an added function, the Toy Hauler compartment usually has folding beds allowing for use as a bedroom. Many will have a second bathroom creating a living space for several more people. The overall length of the RV will determine what features are included and the size of the special compartment.

You will find Toy Haulers in either Travel Trailer or 5th Wheel configurations, suitable for your towing preference. They offer many different floor plans and range in size from 30 feet to over 40 feet, some with triple axel configurations.

Determining the appropriate tow vehicle and hitch configuration can be a little complex with a Toy Hauler. As the weight of the "toys" are added in the special compartment, the actual weight placed on the hitch tongue or 5th wheel king pin will be significantly affected. As with all RV configurations, it is very important to weight the toy hauler both loaded and unloaded to completely understand the towing dynamics.

All of these RV classes and types, except the truck camper, will sleep four comfortably and some are configured for sleeping six. However, the overall living experience and comfort level greatly diminishes with more

14

than two adults. Bunkhouse models provide stacked or bunkbed type of sleeping arrangements which is a great use of limited space. Some models, such as the toy haulers, even come with a sleeping loft, which is fun for the kids to have their own space with windows and a television.

If you plan for a lot of outside entertainment or want to push some of the indoor activities outside, you may be interested in an outdoor kitchen. This usually includes a cooking surface, sink with hot and cold water, small refrigerator and storage for a minimum amount of kitchen supplies. This does significantly add to the RV weight, so consider all of the pros and cons before making your decision on this feature

For many first-time buyers the fear of driving an RV tends to sway them toward shorter units for the perceived less stressful driving experience. You will never learn your driving comfort zone until you give something a try. Test drive a few motorhomes to get the feel of driving something larger than you family automobile.

Frequently you will hear that fifth wheel trailers tow better than a travel trailer and are easier to back up. I have not found this to be true and I think that is because there are many factors that go into how a particular RV will tow.

The wheelbase makes a great difference. This is the distance between the tow vehicle and trailer wheels or in the case of motorhomes, the distance between front wheels and rear wheels. The greater the wheelbase the easier it is to back up and the smoother the overall ride. For example, I have a 12-foot utility trailer which is more difficult to back up than my 27-foot travel trailer.

The other dynamic that is often overlooked is the RV physical design in relation to wind resistance or in other words, is the RV streamlined? Class A motorhomes are a rectangle box with a flat nose. This is probably the worst case in regard to wind resistance and can be difficult to drive under windy conditions. Some travel trailers and fifth wheels have a streamlined nose where others may be a flat surface. The design also plays a significant role in the vehicle's fuel milage.

Pro Tip: Size can make a difference when considering where you will store the RV when not in use. The overall length, height and ground clearance may be a deal breaker if you plan on storing at home.

Gasoline vs Diesel

When considering fuel types for motorhomes (Class A, B or C) or vehicles used for towing trailers, there are currently two choices, gasoline or diesel. Determining the best fuel type is a highly discussed topic with strong proponents on both sides. There are many pros and cons to both fuel types, but the bottom line for making this decision comes down to how and where you intend to travel, how frequently, and of course your financial situation. *Note for clarity: Electric vehicles are not currently a viable option, but this may be changing in the future.*

We are all familiar with gasoline vehicles and we understand (for the most part) what maintenance is required, resale values and the cost of gasoline. We are comfortable with gasoline, and many of you will make a decision purely on your comfort level, and that is completely fine providing you set reasonable expectations.

So, what are these expectations? Things like towing capacity, mountain towing, vehicle fuel economy, refueling frequency, driving comfort and vehicle longevity. We will look at each of these expectations and maybe dispel some of the myths or misunderstanding of these fuel types.

Towing Capacity. Diesel engines provide more power and towing capabilities, and it is not because of the engine size, but a result of the additional torque generated by diesel engines. In simple terms, higher torque produces more strength or power, which is transferred to the drivetrain. As we increase the weight of the RV the need for a diesel vehicle increases. Many will say their gas vehicle can tow a particular weight but that is only part of the complex equation of towing. You also have to consider the vehicle's ability to stop safely with all of that additional weight. And finally, the suspension, transmission, brakes and cooling systems on diesel vehicles are engineered for the demanding conditions associated with towing.

Mountain Towing. A vehicle that is adequate for towing on flat roads may struggle with mountain driving. As described above, the additional engine torque of a diesel engine is much better suited for steep mountain operations. Additionally, many diesel vehicles have an exhaust break or also known as a "Jake" break. This type of break traps the engine pressure in the exhaust system to help reduce the speed of the vehicle without applying the wheel brakes. This prevents the wheel brakes from overheating and excessive break wear.

Fuel Economy. Diesel fuel by volume produces more BTUs, therefore produces more miles per gallon. If gasoline and diesel cost the same per gallon this would be a no brainer considering which fuel is best. Up until just a few years ago diesel was actually cheaper than gasoline. Then in 2006, the EPA regulated the amount of sulfur in diesel to 15 ppm resulting in cost increases to diesel fuel production. Still today, in some limited parts of the United States, diesel is only a few cents more that gasoline. For a high-level cost comparison, fuel economy for recreational vehicles can range from 7mpg for a gas-powered Class A, to over 15mpg for diesel powered Class B coaches or pickup trucks used as a tow vehicle.

Refueling Frequency. With the higher MPG of diesel, the refueling frequency may be extended. And as a RV driver, any time you can avoid pulling into a service station is a good thing. Diesel vehicles typically come standard with larger fuel tanks which results in more miles between fuel stops. Additionally, auxiliary diesel fuel tanks are frequently installed in the bed of pickups to increase their fuel range.

Driving Comfort. Have you ever heard the phrase, "white-knuckle driving?" This is when the driving gets so intense you are gripping the steering wheel as if holding on for dear life. The vehicle's chassis engineering plays a significant role in comfort in terms of suspension and overall drive ability. But all of this is significantly influenced by engine performance, weight distribution and of course, road and weather conditions. And should you ever start to "max out" on towing capacity, engine torque, or road conditions, your driving comfort will deteriorate rapidly. Therefore, if you prefer to stretch the performance of your vehicle, ensure you expectations are set accordingly.

Vehicle Longevity. Ask anyone and they will say a diesel engine will easily last 300,000 miles. The large majority of recreational vehicles will never see 100K miles. In my personal experience, after 12 years of frequent use, we traded our Class A with less that 50K miles. Diesel vehicles typically bring a higher resale price and I feel some of this is because of the higher initial price. I wouldn't be influenced too much with the longevity concern when it comes to making the decision of gasoline or diesel.

At this point you may be thinking that I am encouraging you to take the diesel route, which is not the case. I want you to understand the advantages of both fuel types and to make educated decisions. Let's now take a look at routine maintenance costs which is most owner's concern.

As RV owners, I think most of us understand that doing some of the maintenance yourself will save money. And this is especially true when it comes to the simpler things like oil changes, fuel filters, lubrication and other filters.

Diesel engines usually require more engine oil, and the oil filters may be larger, but I really cannot understand why a diesel oil change can be 3 or 4 times more expensive than for a gas engine. I think this is just a factor of the industry to charge more for diesel service. With that said, it is a completely different case for diesel fuel filters which justifiably are more expensive. Unlike automobiles that can go 50K miles or more between fuel filter changes (some don't even have fuel filters), diesel fuel filters require much more attention. Typically, diesel fuel filters are changed annually and can run several hundred dollars.

This increased cost for routine service tends to discourage some from owning a diesel vehicle. My feeling is that over time the actual cost for diesel service is more, but you get what you pay for. For example, oil change intervals are longer, and the diesel engine doesn't have an electronic ignition system (spark plugs & wires) which can require more periodic maintenance for gas engines, and of course diesels just last longer. However, when an engine failure occurs, diesel repairs will be more expensive, in particular when considering the modern engines with diesel exhaust fluid (DEF) systems and diesel participant filters (DPF).

If a diesel is "required" for your application, purchase what is needed to get the job done. Understand your vehicle needs and research all solutions and you will arrive at the correct decision for you.

Notes:

The Buying Process

You have already visited all of the local RV dealerships and maybe traveled out of town or out of state and you have now settled on a dealer. If possible, I would work my top two dealers against each other and just maybe this can increase your buying leverage. Complete your homework, organize your notes, and have a buying strategy ready when moving into the buying phase.

Buying Strategy

Your buying strategy is a mental condition (write it down if necessary) on what you want, what you can afford, what you are willing to compromise. The goal is to get to a happy place where your needs are filled, and you feel good about it. The feeling good part is particularly important and if you don't have it you may need to walk away and consider other options.

We all want the killer deal, and the seller wants the maximum profits, so the trick is to find a sweet point in which everyone is happy or at least feels good about the purchase. There are many variables to consider and everything seems to be thrown out the window if you have a trade, so I'll approach this from a straight up deal with no trade.

If you do have a trade, an honest dealer will let you know up front that by selling the trade yourself could bring a higher price than what the dealer will allow in trade value. Some online resources for selling an RV is RV Trader (fee based), Facebook Market Place and Craig's List. Be aware there are many scams with online sales, approach with caution and if the deal looks too good then it probably is not authentic. Selling on consignment is another option which authorizes a dealer or lot to sell the RV with a seller's commission.

The utopia of RV bargaining from the buyer's perspective is to take 30 percent off the MSRP, add document fees (what the dealer gets for their administrative efforts), transportation costs (usually standard charge for shipping the unit regardless of geographical location) and taxes. But it never quite happens that way, however the 30% is a good target. There are two caveats on discounts.

(1) as seen in 2020 with a huge upturn of RV sales, discounts are reduced as available inventory is reduced and

(2) some brands hold higher resale values and discounts max out at or under 20-23 percent with Airstream being one brand that comes to mind.

Buying Pre-Owned

Buying a pre-owned unit requires special knowledge and experience to determine the condition of the RV structure and operation of the components and systems. The major concern for pre-owned units is moisture collection and water damage. To the untrained eye everything may appear fine when in fact the underlying structure can contain mold, rotting wood or decaying particle board and possible delamination of the outside surface material. Always hire a professional NRVIA (National RV Inspector's Association) Inspector to inspect and evaluate a pre-owned RV before you sign a contract.

Internet Shopping

The Internet has changed the way we shop including large expensive items like an RV. Almost all RV dealers will have an Internet website where you can compare models, brands and prices. And you will quickly see four or five major nation-wide dealerships attempting to corner the market on RV sales. Leverage all this knowledge as best you can but don't be fooled by the fancy website with flashy photos and 3D virtual tour videos and certainly don't lock in on any of the prices just yet.

If you haven't already done so, this is the time to visit several if not all of the local area RV dealerships to start the process of finding that perfect RV.

Pro Tip: The dealer is motivated to sell the inventory sitting on their lot for many reasons. They will push those units and offer discounts which may be good or maybe not so good. Each unit will have a date of manufacture posted on the weight and load label on the outside of the unit. Consider how long the RV has sat on the RV lot, how many people may have strolled into the RV working each cabinet and drawer, twisting the faucet knobs, and peeking into the storage compartments. Believe it or not this adds to the wear and tear. How often did the dealer vacuum the sand out of the carpet? Finally, just sitting in the weather for several months starts to reduce the life of caulk, weather seals and the overall roofing material. All of this is leverage you have when making the final deal.

Special Order

The final option to consider is ordering an RV from the manufacturer. Dealers will place an order for a unit with the specific model, colors, and options you desire. The wait time to delivery can range from weeks to several months depending on brands and time of year. Keep in mind that since the unit is not already on the dealer's lot any price discounts will be minimized. I have special ordered in the past and was pleased with the results but as you may see it is not for everyone.

Other Considerations

In the current seller's market dealers really want to make deals but in many cases the lack of inventory stands in the way. This is not good for you or the dealer and it puts stress on the entire system from manufacturer to consumer. In my opinion neither party should take advantage of the other. Meaning as a buyer don't expect past historical levels of discounts and the sellers should not get greedy. There is plenty of market for everyone providing buyers are willing to either accept the current prices or wait for inventory to replenish. I guess the key is to employ your best negotiating skills and stay focused on your buying strategy.

Add-ons such as dealer installed options, hitches, tow bars and extended warranty programs can significantly add to the bottom line. It is always best to know up front what you need and understand the final sales price as early as possible.

Ensure your dealer installed options or other towing equipment is available and guaranteed for delivery. Frequently dealers have a standard brand of items such as hitches and tow bars they sell. Customers asking for a different brand may be told a product can be obtained only to find out upon delivery it is not available, and must settle for the dealer's brand.

Extended Warranties

Extended warranties are not for everyone primally because of price, conditions for coverage and limitations. It is nothing more than insurance, which is a promise to provide funds for specific failures that fall within their conditions and limitations. All I'll suggest here is that you do not have to make this decision on the day you purchase the RV. Usually the quoted price is good for 30 to 90 days. Go home and think about it, do some online research for similar coverages, and try to find reviews from customers that have purchased and used the same warranty package.

Notes:

A Good Maintenance Relationship

Buying local verses going for a cheaper deal out of town or out of state demands considerable thought. Larger dealers will offer lower prices and from a financial perspective it may be the best deal available. But keep in mind that the sale is only half, if that much, of the total experience of purchasing an RV. The sale is a two- or three-day event. Where on the other hand obtaining professional RV service will follow you every day for the life of your RV. Good service which is reasonably priced and somewhat convenient may be difficult to find.

RV service is unlike automobile service in many ways. And the most significant difference is that a RV service facility that **did not sell you the RV** are under no obligation to perform warranty service or any service. Even if a dealership sells the exact same brand and model you have, they may be "too busy" to perform your warranty work if you did not purchase from that dealer. That's just a fact of the RV industry.

If you haven't guessed it yet, a good service relationship may prove to be more valuable in the long run than the selling discount offered a few hundred miles down the road. Consider the time and expense involved if you travel several hundred miles for service. By the way, where do you stay while the service is being conducted? I'm not recommending you avoid those out-of-town opportunities, just suggesting you consider all the pros and cons before jumping on a cheaper deal.

A quick look at a dealer's service lot will provide a picture of how many units are awaiting service. Ask about wait times for service, wait times on parts and how many service bays are available. Try to get the best feel you can on how you will be treated when it comes time to service your RV.

You may find that making any service visit is too time consuming or not convenient to your schedule. In this case I would search for a RV Mobile Service Tech. Mobile service is becoming more popular not only for convenience but for people like me I want to watch the service being performed to give me some level of confidence and comfort.

Mobile techs are usually authorized to perform warranty service. There will be additional coordination with the manufacturer necessary to obtain authorization for labor reimbursements and parts. The owner may be responsible for the initial service call fee which can be between 100 and 200 dollars.

Finding an RV mobile tech can be a challenge. The best place to check is with campground management. Often the campgrounds will know who is available locally and who does good work.

> **Pro Tip**: When you do find a good RV service provider give them praise and good reviews. Let others know when you have a good service experience. Also let them know when it didn't go so well. Maybe we can't make a bad service provider improve, but we can help potential customers find a better provider.

Notes:

Short Lesson on RV Weights

The Number one most asked question about buying an RV is about weight specifications. But surprisingly there are many buyers who don't investigate the issue of RV weight until **after they have made the purchase**. Please don't be one of these poor unfortunate souls because it will cost you money and who knows it may cost someone's life.

Be very careful of any suggestions that your vehicle can tow a particular trailer without first considering the actual weights involved and the manufacture's tow weights and capacities. The frequent statement that your truck can tow anything on the lot is a sure path to heartbreak when you find otherwise.

Each vehicle manufactured in the United States has a Tire and Loading Information sticker either on the driver side front door post or on the outside front left corner of the RV. These weights are used to determine the Dry Wight and Gross Vehicle Weight Rating keeping in mind these are estimates.

Each vehicle and trailer will be different and should not be generalized when determining the appropriate and safe towing configurations. As a industry standard, do not exceed 80 percent of stated towing capacities.

Dry Weight
The weight of the RV without any liquids, passengers, or cargo. New units are weighed by the manufacturers as they come off the assembly line. It is like to Curb Weight for automobiles.

Gross Vehicle Weight (GVW)
The RV Dry Weight plus all added content such as liquids, cargo and passengers.

Gross Vehicle Weight Rating (GVWR)

This is the maximum allowable weight of an RV. The Gross Vehicle Weight should not exceed the Gross Vehicle Weight Rating.

Gross Combined Vehicle Weight Rating (GCVWR)

The maximum weight of both the tow vehicle and its trailer combined. This weight is obtained by weighing the tow vehicle and trailer when hitched together.

Tow Rating

The manufacturer's rating of the maximum weight limit that can safely be towed by a specific vehicle. As a rule, limit trailer weight to 80 percent of the specified tow rating weight.

Tongue Weight or Pin Weight

The weight placed on the tow vehicle (trailer hitch or fifth wheel hitch) when the trailer is hitched to tow vehicle.

Payload or Cargo Carrying Capacity (CCC)

The difference from the Dry Weight and the Gross Vehicle Weight Rating. In the case of a tow vehicle, the Payload is the weight that is added to the vehicle's Dry Weight such as passengers, pets and cargo. Always include the actual hitch which may add several hundred pounds in the case of fifth wheels.

As a note of caution, if your vehicle's payload capacity is exceeded, there is nothing you can add or modify to increase the payload. This includes rear suspension air bags or modifications to the springs. This reenforces the recommendation to thoroughly investigate all weights and towing capacities before purchasing an Airstream or tow vehicle.

There are online resources that will calculate safe towing configurations and can be extremely helpful when shopping for a tow vehicle. To be on the safe side I recommend shopping for the trailer first then shop for a tow vehicle that will be fully capable to tow within specifications.

Pro Tip: This book provides only a small glimpse into RV weight concerns and is not a definitive narrative on how to calculate or evaluate towing specifications. Do your homework and research the details thoroughly and once you do get on the road with the new RV go to a commercial scale and weigh it yourself.

Taking Delivery

The fun and learning shifts into high gear at this point. The Pre-Delivery Inspection or PDI is a standard event which allows the customer to do a detailed inspection and operational orientation prior to accepting the RV. It is also a great opportunity to start taking notes or even making a video. Yes, this is done prior to writing the check and signing on the dotted line. In fact, this is the last opportunity you have to call off the deal and walk away realizing that you may lose your down payment. I can't stress how important the PDI is for you to learn about the RV and to ensure it functions as advertised. Everything should be working and looking extremely good at this point; and if not immediately express your concern and request resolution prior to proceeding with the purchasing transaction.

Don't Leave the Lot

Okay, go ahead and consider me picky or marginally OCD but I always let the dealer know up front that I will be spending at least the first night camping on the dealer's lot. I have stayed on the lot following a RV purchase three times and it is not unusual to ask for an electrical hookup and water for one night.

Spend that first night using everything in the RV and I mean everything. Take showers, cook, wash dishes, put out the awning, run the AC and furnace, microwave, TV, DVD player and the list goes on. Keep a list of what doesn't work and what you don't understand. The next morning give the list to the service department or sales representative for resolution.

I wouldn't leave the lot until everything is fixed because once you leave you become just "another customer" which gets you a place at the rear of the service line. You have some leverage as a new delivery customer so take full advantage of it.

Conducting the PDI (Pre-Delivery Inspection)

Don't rush the delivery process and take your time conducting the PDI. After all dealers charge for this inspection/orientation session and usually have a sales contract line item for several hundred dollars to cover the PDI. Additionally, do not take delivery in the dark or when it's raining. Bad weather and darkness will force you to rush through the inspection and you will miss items that may require attention.

If physically able I recommend using a ladder to look at the roof and visually inspecting the caulk and all seals as best you can. Ensure there are no cracks in vent hoods, skylights and the plastic holding tank vent covers. Look for protruding screws and nails that could puncture the roofing material. If you can't make the climb to the roof ask the dealership to take your camera and snap a few photos or shoot a brief video.

From each outside corner of the RV put your head close to the surface and view across the outside surface looking for bubbles, bulges, waves or other anormal surface conditions. These are indicators of delamination or separation of the outside skin from the interior structure. Also look underneath for any loose screws, molding or anything just looking out of place.

> **Pro Tip**: You are paying for the delivery inspection and it is not over until you say it's over. Should the dealer representative say something is "normal" when your gut feeling tells you otherwise, ask to see the same thing on a different RV for comparison. Meet the Service Manager to discuss your expectations for future service and don't forget to get his/her business card for future reference.

We all have seen the 15-page checklist for the pre-delivery inspection and frankly I'm not sure a long-detailed checklist is the best approach. After all you will be overly excited seeing and touching your new RV and thinking about just getting out on the road. Very quickly you will either start to bond with the dealer representative performing the PDI and you will probably put more trust in them than you should. My advice is to be a sceptic and always be from Missouri having the "Show Me" attitude.

With that said, here is a short checklist keeping in mind you want to see and operate everything in the RV.

Outside
- Walk around outside touching and opening all panels and compartments
- Look at the underside for any loose objects, trim or electrical wiring
- All windows on the outside look normal without blemishes
- On the roof look for uncaulked seams or cracked or broken caulk and seals
- View all outside panels as described above

Inside
- Operate all appliances including LP and Electric if so equipped
- Run every faucet and shower with cold and hot water
- Look for water leaks under and inside cabinets, around shower and toilet
- Open every drawer and cabinet, ensure knobs and handles are secure
- All lights work, test the switches
- Find the GFCI and ask how to operate
- Open and close all doors and windows
- Open and close sleeper sofa
- Heating works on LP furnace and on Heat Pump if equipped
- Air conditioning work on all units
- Inspect the ceiling for any water marks, sags, or loose coverings
- Inspect the flooring for bumps, bubbles, or loose seams

Final Check
- LP Tanks are full
- Batteries Charged, ask how to maintain batteries
- Tires set to correct tire pressure

- Spare Tire secured if equipped

Learning the entertainment system and automated control panels (if equipped) can be complex but important. Again, take your time, take notes and photos, and don't stop until you feel comfortable.

Notes:

First Night Camping

Whoo-hoo, you are on the way; cruising down the road probably a little exhausted maybe even overwhelmed but the adrenalin has kicked in and you are pumped. You've made plans to camp close to home or maybe you purchased your RV out of state, so you'll be looking for a campground in the first 50 to 100 miles. Use that first driving opportunity to get the feel of driving or towing and don't go too far that first day just in case you need to make a return visit to the dealer for an emergency repair.

If you go home that first night, I recommend you camp in the driveway or yard so you can continue the learning process. If you are unable to store your RV at home, I would highly recommend spending a few days at a campground to learn about your electrical system and how the battery is charged and plan on how you will keep the battery charged while in storage. More information on this later but I will say that frequently new RV owners will let their battery or batteries run down resulting in battery replacement and in some cases replacing what were new batteries.

A common mistake I see is taking delivery in mid-winter and placing the Airstream in storage before it has ever been used. This sets the stage for the new owner to start from ground zero and have to learn everything again from the beginning. This is just one of the important reasons why camping immediately upon purchase is stressed, and maybe stressed more than once in this book.

Hopefully, you spent the very first night camping on the dealer's lot so you could operate and check everything thoroughly. If you did, you are feeling confident about operating all the appliances along with the electrical and water systems. Keep taking notes as you learn more about each component and become more familiar with your new home.

Establish a routine on how you can react to emergencies. Find the fire extinguisher, read the instructions, and discuss with your family how you will respond to a fire. Practice an emergency evacuation from the RV. Know where the emergency exits are and know how to open the exits. RV fires can quickly consume the entire unit and in most situations, evacuation is the best plan.

Test the smoke and LP/Propane detectors. Know how to turn off the Propane tanks should the alarm activate. Teach everyone how to operate the door lock to prevent being locked inside should an emergency arise.

As you spend this first night in the RV investigate every compartment, cabinet, under sitting areas and any other space that may have electrical or plumbing components. Learn the various noises made by the water pump, converter and be diligent in watching for water leaks.

> **Pro Tip:** Start reading the manufactures documentation. I say start because it may take some time to work your way through the very dry and boring details. Become familiar with the specifications such as holding tank capacities, overall RV height, battery type and operating limits for inverters. Learn how to keep the batteries charged by shore power, solar or battery chargers. Finally, complete any warranty activation on appliances including air conditioners, some of these may have an activation deadline.

Use your first night camping to start recording what you need to outfit your new RV. Later in this book is a list of the Top Ten Essential Items for a New RV and Tools for Travel and the Campsite.

I hope your RV dealer gave you some freebies to get you started and some dealers do offer a complimentary starter kit. But there are always items needed for a new RV. Let's get that list started now and I'll give you a hand.

1. First Aid Kit
2. Bug Spray
3. Flashlight
4. Cleaning Supplies

5. …
6. …
7. …
8. …
9. …
10. …

Jack Hunnicutt

Part II

You learn more from failure than from success. Don't let it stop you. Failure builds character.

~Unknown

Stephen C. Foster State Park - Okefenokee Swamp Georgia

Campground Driving and Parking

Slow down, the Speed Limit is 5 to 10 MPH. This is because the campground access road can be very narrow and frequently in disrepair with potholes, loose gravel and possibly mud. It is not unusual to find vehicles parked on both sides of the road limiting the space you must navigate, so be careful. It may be helpful if pulling a TOAD to unhook at the registration office.

You would think campground managers would be experts in tree trimming or at least know when to call in the professionals to do the job, but this is not always the case. Low hanging limbs can and will damage your Airstream. Even what you may consider small bushes or limbs can crush a body panel costing hundreds of dollars, if not more, to repair. Taking an extra minute or two navigating into the campsite may save you a lot of heartache and money.

Approach the Campsite

If a map of the campground is provided upon check become familiar with the best route to your campsite. How you approach the campsite makes a huge difference in parking. The camp attendant should provide specific directions on approaching your site. Remember to be thinking ahead trying to avoid any surprises when you pull up to the campsite.

Stop in front of the campsite, get out and do a walk around looking for obstacles, low handing limbs, trees that will interfere with extending your slides or awning and most importantly know exactly when the water, sewer and electrical connects are located.

While doing the initial campsite evaluation ask yourself the following questions:

1. Is the roof clear of all limbs and any limbs that potentially could fall? Especially after a storm check for broken limbs simply waiting to fall.

2. Can the slide(s) extend and leave room for the awning? Leave plenty of room to hookup utilities.

3. Is the power cord, water hose and sewer hose long enough to reach the connection? It doesn't hurt to carry extensions for all of these.

4. Is the site level, front to back and left to right? Frequently you can eyeball a sloping surface and determine if additional leveling steps are necessary.

5. Will the storage compartment doors open completely and clear of any obstacles?

6. Is the fire ring too close to the RV? I have seen fire rings placed within 3 feet of the RV which is not enough clearance for safety.

7. Should there be a hard rain where will the water drain? Too often we see in the news of campgrounds flooding and recreational vehicles being washed away. Never hurts to be aware of your surroundings.

Backing Strategy

Walk back to your vehicle or motorhome and look in all directions sizing up your backing strategy. Understand than when backing your front wheels will track very wide and may run off the road so be aware of culverts, ditches and small marker signs that may be in the way. If parked vehicles are in the way politely ask the owner to temporarily move the vehicle. Fellow campers will understand and do what they can to assist.

Pull head allowing the rear wheels of the RV to come just past the campsite entrance. I usually go another 3 or 4 feet past the entrance to start my backing alignment. Motorhomes are like backing an automobile just making wider turns allowing the extreme butt end of the unit ample space to clear any obstacles.

Trailers will present more of a challenge since the trailer responds completely backwards when backing. I recommend **placing your hands on the bottom of the steering wheel** (Four and Eight O'clock) so that when you turn the wheel the trailer's butt end will go in the same direction as your hands. You may have to pull forward a time or two to realign your vehicles. Go very slowly and making minor corrections to your path until you are completely parked.

The Key to Backing

The key to backing an RV is practice. No one nails the backing process the first time, or the second or third time. If it takes you several attempts DO NOT WORRY ABOUT IT, just do what is necessary to stay safe. Trust me, everyone else in the campground that may be watching has been in your shoes. Personally, I try not to watch and just go about my business, should the driver need assistance they will ask. If you need assistance don't hesitate to ask.

> **Pro Tip**: If you have a Co-pilot have that person watch or direct from the rear of the RV and have them stay visible in your mirrors so you can see their signals. Using a walkie talkie is helpful but a good set of hand signals should be sufficient. The most important signal is to STOP before hitting an obstacle.

Departing the Campground

It goes without saying don't be the one dragging a sewer or water hose behind the RV as you are departing the campground. Secure everything well and don't forget to look under the RV for any loose items that have not been properly secured.

When it's time to depart the campground know exactly how to drive to the exit or how to get to the dump station if you did not have a sewer connection. You will find that most of the campground internal roads are one way which facilitates backing into the campsites.

Approach the dump site from the correct direction to place the sewer connection on the driver's side of the RV. Align the sewer connection of the RV and the dump connection to keep the hose as straight and as short as possible. This will make for a quicker clean up and easier storage of the hoses.

Do not get rushed at the dump station even if you have people waiting in line. But don't take you sweet time either, know what you are doing and just get it done. You may want to pull away from the dump station a short distance and go through your "ready to drive" checklist and ensure you and the passengers are completely ready before driving off.

Notes:

Unhitching and Setup

For all the lucky travel trailer or fifth wheel owners the dealer has installed your hitch and performed the setup making everything simply perfect. They even hitched you all up and gave clear directions for you to follow. Maybe you took a few notes, a photo or two just in case for later use. It's now time to see how well your memory or notes are working. Go ahead and unhitch that monster.

There are several different hitch configurations so it will not be possible for me to provide detailed step by step directions. I can however, provide some general guidance to help stimulate your memory and work you through the process.

Safety first and safety always. Don't do anything without first thinking through the process and clearly understanding what the next step will be and the next step and so on and on. With the trailers (TT and 5th wheels) they are secure and stable while attached to the tow vehicle, but the moment they become separated the trailer will respond to gravity and roll if not properly wheel chocked and secured.

Unhitching Routine

An established routine is essential and can be aided by use of a checklist. Try to avoid distractions and stay focused until the job is complete. This is no time for a friendly neighbor to strike up a conversation and tell you what a beautiful RV you have. Either stop your job completely and have the conversation or ask them to come back later.

In overly broad terms the unhitching and setup process will look something like the following.

- Secure the vehicles (motorhome or trailers) with chocks.
- Perform unhitching process for trailers.

- Connect shore power if available, this will assist your batteries when setting up.
- Level the RV, again this will vary depending on RV and manual or automated leveling.
- Put down stabilizers.
- Enter the RV and secure items that became unseated during travel (pillows, chairs etc.).
- Extend slides, best to have someone outside to check slide clearance when extending.
- Complete hooking up utilities, "clean things" first then the "dirty things." More on this in a later chapter.
- Inside, verify water pressure and electrical power.
- Ensure refrigerator is operating on correct mode (LP or Electric), set HVAC thermostat and activate water heater.
- All done.

This is not your checklist; these are the high-level expected actions and not the precise "how to" steps in an order specific to your RV. If you are going to use a checklist develop your own by walking through the process and recording the detailed actions. After you have conducted the setup a few times you will do it all from memory. That is until next season when you will have forgotten about half of the critical steps. So, keep the checklist handy until you can perform it in your sleep.

Campsite Setup

Setting up your RV will certainly get easier over time and you will change your process as you become better and start to learn time saving and more efficient tricks from fellow campers. If you are boondocking or dry camping the actual setup will not be much more than the unhitching process. Some further discussion is necessary to better understand campground utilities and how best to take advantage of these services.

Electrical

Electric service will be provided in 30-amp, 50-amp, or both and typically the power pedestal will also have a 15-amp outlet. Turn off the breaker before plugging in your power cord. Plug in the cord then flip the breaker to the ON position. Use of a good surge protector is highly recommended. Once you access my Facebook Group or Blog you will learn more about specific surge protector models and the advantages of one over the other.

Plugs with a loose connection will generate heat and eventually scorch or melt the plug requiring the plug to be replaced or in extreme cases it can create a fire. Frequently campsite pedestal plugs become stressed from excessive usage and the plug does not make solid contact on all of the prongs. This is usually the case with 30-amp plugs. If you experience this use your 50-amp adapter and plug in to the 50-amp receptacle for a better connection and it may prevent damaging your plug.

Water

City Water in the campground is usually well water especially in rural areas. The water is potable or considered drinking water, yet you may want to use a water filter. Use either a disposable inline filter on the water hose or a filtering system installed in your RV. Aside from the obvious benefits of a filter it can also prevent sand and other small particles from invading your RV plumbing and eventually causing problems. It is also a good idea to use a water pressure regulator to protect the plumbing components from high pressure water. A setting of 40 to 50 psi will provide sufficient pressure for showers and flushing while not over taxing the plumbing.

Sewer

Sewer connections are not found at all campgrounds especially state and national parks. If connections are not available at the campsite there will usually be a dump station available. Most commercial campgrounds and RV resorts provide a sewer connection at each campsite with few exceptions. A sewer hose reaching 10 to 20 feet should be sufficient for most campgrounds.

To conclude with the campsite setup, refer to your RV documentation for connecting TV antenna and Cable service. At a minimum the TV will require a channel scan and for Cable setup remember to turn off the antenna amplifier.

Pro Tip: Even with a sewer connection at the campsite do not leave the gray or black tank valves open. Doing so may allow sewer gas, bugs, rats, and other things to enter you holding tanks. Dump the gray as needed then close the valve. Allow the black tank to fill until 2/3 full then flush and again close the valve. This is such an important issue you will find this same recommendation in other sections of this book.

Notes:

Part III

Confidence is not "they will like me." Confidence is "I'll be fine if they don't."

~Christina Crimme

Rest, Relax and Replenish - Interstate 20

RV Holding Tanks

Maybe you think learning about your wastewater should be tucked away in a later chapter after exploring the more "exciting" aspects of RV ownership. There are few things more exciting than taking a shower and seeing brown water coming up from the drain; and that is why we need to cover these potential trouble areas first.

You have three types of holding tanks, freshwater, gray water, and black water. In rare cases two or more tanks of the same type. For example, larger fifth wheels and units with multiple bathrooms may have 2 gray water tanks. Check your RV documentation to learn your specific setup. However, the discussion that follows will apply regardless of tank configuration.

Fresh Water Tank

Drinking or potable water, which is supplied to sinks and toilets from either the Fresh Water holding tank or from the City Water hose connection. You have the option of leaving the freshwater tank empty. The advantages of carrying onboard water is having toilet flush water when on the road between campsites or when fresh water is not available at the campsite, such as when dry camping or boondocking.

Avoid storing fresh water longer than a few weeks to prevent the water from turning stale and possibly start growing algae and mold. Drain and flush the tank with fresh water and a half-cup of bleach or vinegar for every 20 gallons of water. Rinse thoroughly before restoring your fresh water supply.

When filling the freshwater tank ensure the water is potable and if possible, use a water filter. Water outlets at dump sites are not potable and are for rinsing tanks and not drinking.

When city water is not available the fresh water in the holding tank uses the water pump to pressurize the water making it flow to the faucets, shower and toilet. The water pump is operated by 12v DC and it makes a very distinctive nose when in operation. Turn the pump off when not in use.

Gray Water Tank

Water draining from sinks and shower. It is called gray because the soap residue turns the water gray. Avoid letting any oils or food particles wash down the sink drains to prevent possible tank blockage.

The gray tank will take care of itself and does not require an additive or chemical treatment. However, the gray tank can produce odors if not properly vented. It is also important to keep water in the sink and shower traps to prevent odor coming up from the tank.

Black Water Tank

Toilet waste and the associated wastewater is usually brown but referred to as black water. As you can image the water will have waste particles and toilet paper residue which if not properly managed and treated can result in tank blockage, odors and costly repairs.

There are many home remedy solutions for black tank management. However, I only have confidence in professional products and best practices that have served me well over the years.

- **Toilet Paper.** I have had good luck using any paper marked "Septic Safe." With this said I don't recommend using the thicker multi-ply soft stuff. The key here is to flush with plenty of water making sure everything in the Black Tank is completely covered with water without an opportunity to dry out. When "things" dry in the tank the particles get hard eventually create a clog or stoppage.

- **Black Tank Treatment.** Use a proven quality treatment and avoid the home remedy solutions; one day you will thank me for this. I use and recommend Happy Campers Holding Tank Treatment.

- **Back Flush.** If your RV is equipped with a Black Tank Flush connection use it every time you dump the tank. This flushing removes any particles left in the tank and helps to ensure against poop buildup and the dreaded *Poop Pyramid.*

- **Never Flush Items.** Paper towels, Handy Wipes, female hygiene products, toilet paper not marked "Septic Safe." Just because something says "disposable" does not mean you can or should flush it.

Water Pump

The water pump is only necessary when using water from the fresh water holding tank when city water is not available. When connected to city water, keep the water pump turned off. These pumps operate on 12v power, are very reliable, and should last many years. However, there are situations when the pump may require attention.

- **Loss of Prime**. This may happen when retuning the pump to service after it has been winterized. Although the pumps are self-priming, they may require some help in establishing the prime. This is achieved by removing the strainer cap (clear plastic bulb) and pouring a small amount of water into the pump.

- **Uneven Water Flow**. The strainer can collect debris such as small participles of sand which interfere with water flow. The water pump strainer can be removed and rinsed with clean water to clear the obstruction.

- **Fresh Water Tank Overfills**. When connected to city water there should not be any water going into the fresh water holding tank. If the tank does fill, and you don't know why, it is most likely a stuck or dirty check valve in the water pump. Try turning off the city water connection and use the water from the fresh water holding tank. This may clear the backflow value after cycling the pump on and off several times. If this does not correct the issue you may have to remove the water pump head and clean the inside check valve. Refer to your pump's documentation for details since this is a general solution and may be different for your specific

51

pump.

- **Pump Does Not Stop Running**. This could be caused by a leak in the line or connections which allow air to be drawn into the system. Or in some cases the water pump requires adjustment. Again, consult you pump documentation for details on making adjustments.

Holding Tank Sensors

I have heard many excuses explaining why it is common for holding tank sensors to not accurately display or to fail completely. The most common is the owner's failure to properly flush and rinse the tanks especially for the black water holding tank. I can buy the black tank issue but in general I think the sensors are engineered for a cheap solution. All I can recommend is to get a good feel for how much water is being used and approximate when to do your next dump. The early warning signs of full or approaching full tanks are:

- gurgling or unusual noise from the plumbing or underbelly
- dirty water backing up in the lowest drain, usually the shower
- visually seeing "stuff" in the black tank when flushing toilet
- water dripping from the underbelly

For many reasons it is not unusual for holding tank indicators that display holding tank status to not be accurate or not work at all.

> **Pro Tip:** Keep all holding tank valves closed until you are ready to dump. Even if you have a sewer connection at your campsite. Keep the valves closed else unwanted critters like rats, gnats, sewer flies and of course sewer gas can come up into your holding tanks.
> o Fill the black tank to 2/3 full before flushing.
> o Dump the Black Tank first, do the black tank flush, and lastly, flush the gray tank.
> o Flushing the gray tank last will rinse out the sewer hose and reduce odor while in storage.

I'm a firm believer in being proactive whenever possible and that is a common thread throughout this book. In the case of holding tanks, don't assume everyone is aware of how holding tanks operate. Inform all guests of the never flush items identified above and don't let children play in the bathroom. That missing toy or hair comb could cost hundreds of dollars to extract from the holding tank.

Notes:

Fresh Water Do's and Don'ts

Cross-contamination between fresh water (drinking water) components and the hoses and fitting used for wastewater can be a health risk. Just being aware of these concerns is half the battle of maintaining an acceptable level of sanitation. Incorporating these steps into your setup process can help ensure you keep your fresh water fresh and safe.

- When doing the RV setup do all "clean" activities first. Fresh water hose and filter, electrical connection, jack, slides.
- Leave the "dirty" setup for last. Connect and extend the sewer hose.
- Keep a spray bottle of 9 parts to 1 bleach water mix. Spray the water faucet and hose ends before connecting.
- Do not use the freshwater hose to back flush the black water holding tank. Use a different hose preferably with a different color. I have a gray colored hose for this.
- Store the freshwater components in a plastic container with lid. This includes the drinking water hose, water filter, water pressure regulator and a special hose for filling the freshwater tank (if required).
- Sewer hoses and fitting are stored in a separate container or location.

Hose Storage

Some RV manufactures do a much better job than others when it comes to sewer hose storage solutions. If you do not have designated sewer hose storage in either a bumper, attached to the underbelly or in a wet storage area you will have to be creative in forming your own solution. A plastic container with a sealed lid approximately 20" by 24" and 6" deep may be sufficient for a 10' sewer hose and attachments.

I keep a similar size plastic container for all of all my freshwater hoses, filters, and water pressure regulator. This is also where I keep a spray bottle with the bleach water solution. And even with all this segregation of "clean and dirty" components it is not a perfect system. Just think about how many times your water hose was lying on the ground next to or even on top of the sewer hose.

> **Pro Tip:** When setting up at the campsite try not to let the freshwater hose touch the ground. This may be possible by hanging the hose on the power pedestal or placing your plastic container on the ground with the hose coiled on top of the container. Placing the hose on the ground close to the sewer hose may not be avoidable but try.

Campsite Water

Campsite water is suitable for drinking unless campground management has informed you differently. Using a water filter can add some protection and improve the taste however there is no guarantee every campground will have good drinking water. Therefore, it is especially important to visually check the condition of the water coming from the faucet before connecting your hose. Let the water run for 20 to 30 seconds and the water should appear to be clear, if it looks cloudy, brown, or yellow have campground management check the water.

Precautions such as these may be stated more than once in this book to stress their importance and to make sure you get the message. Sorry for the redundancy but few things in your Airstream are more important than clean safe drinking water.

Take some bottled water even if you don't plan to use bottled water. You may find yourself in a situation where the only suitable drinking water is what you brought.

Each campsite sees many campers over time; hundreds in just one year is possible and likely. It only takes one camper to accidentally spill sewage or rinse their sewer hose onto the ground to contaminate the campsite for a long period. Being considerate to other campers and the environment goes a long way in keeping fresh water safe for everyone.

Refer to Campground Etiquette for more on acceptable campground behavior.

Notes:

Electrical Systems

It is best to think about electricity in your RV as two separate systems, Direct Current (DC – 12v) and Alternating Current (AC – 110v) or in RV lingo, shore power. The two systems are separate because some appliances and components operate on DC power while others require AC power. In the chapter covering appliances you will learn that some appliances can operate on either AC or DC with propane depending upon which power source is available or desired.

Shore Power (AC)

Electrical power provided by the campground and found on the power pedestal in either 30-amp or 50-amp electrical outlet. To determine the amperage rating of your RV just remember that 3 prongs on the power plug indicates 30-amps while 4 prongs are 50-amps.

Converter

The converter is powered by 110v Shore Power (or Generator Power) and converts 110v to 12v DC and charges your battery. Smart converters have a multi-stage battery charger which will not over-charge your battery. Also, modern generation converters can power the DC devices even if the RV does not have a battery installed; traditional converters require a battery to provide any DC power to the RV.

Inverter

Is directly connected to the battery and transforms 12v DC to 110v AC power. Typically, the Inverter (if installed) is wired to designated 110v outlets in the RV. Some RVs have residential refrigerators which are AC only and require an Inverter to operate when shore power is not available.

The Inverter is frequently confused with the Converter. One way to remember their differences is with the Converter think of it as a Charger, both start with a "C." Charging the battery is the primary purpose of the

Converter. On the other hand, the Inverter actually "Invents" alternating current from the battery. Notice I have used the letter "I" to connect Inverter with Invents. Inverters are really not necessary at all unless you do not have shore power or generator power AND you want to use 110v from the wall outlets. Still confused? Do this, keep the Inverter turned OFF all the time unless you are actually boondocking or dry camping and you may want to put a label on the Inverter switch saying, "Dry Camping Only."

Battery Power (DC)

Stores 12v DC power. Batteries have many configurations, single, multiple, 6v, 12v. Battery types are Lead Acid and Lithium. Lead acids include Flooded Lead Acid, Absorbed Glass Mat (AGM), Sealed, and Gel. The Flooded Lead Acid are the highest maintenance battery requiring the water level to be maintained periodically.

All RV batteries are Deep Cycle meaning the battery can be discharged and recharged (charge cycle) many more times than a traditional automotive battery and recharge more quickly. Under no circumstances should a Lead Acid battery ever be discharged below 50 percent capacity.

Lithium batteries are extremely expensive in comparison to Lead Acid batteries. However, Lithium batteries weigh much less and can be totally discharged without any damage to the battery. AGM or Lithium are recommended for RVs with solar power systems.

Breaker and Fuse

All electrical circuits (appliances & outlets) are protected from high voltage surges by using Breakers and Fuses. Become familiar with your Breaker Panel and have spare fuses on hand if needed. There may also be inline fuses and breakers for jacks, slides and other components.

Solar Power

Solar is nothing more than a battery charger and, is typically less than 200 watts in capacity. This is an excellent way to maintain the battery when not connected to shore power. RV solar power will never support high amperage usages such as microwave oven, air conditioning, hair dryer or electric space heater.

Battery Disconnect Switch

Most units come with a Battery Disconnect Switch to protect the batteries when the RV is not connected to shore power. This switch is usually wired to disconnect 12v DC power to most devices; please note this is most devices but not everything. Even when the switch is engaged some devices such as the smoke and LP detectors and entertainment systems with a clock will continue to drain power from the batteries. Additionally, depending on how it is wired the disconnect switch may prevent solar charging with the switch engaged.

GFCI

Ground Fault Circuit Interrupter (GFCI) outlets are located both inside and outside of the RV. These outlets provide a safety breaker to protect the user in areas that contain water like the bathroom, kitchen and out of doors. Should the GFCI trip, all outlets on the circuit will be inoperable. The control GFCI breaker may be on one of the outlets or in the RV main breaker panel.

Additionally, GFCI outlets are subject to tripping when exposed to moisture. This includes extremely high humidity and exposure to rain on the outside outlets. If moisture is the cause of your GFCI problem, you can use a hair dryer on the low setting to blow warm dry air into the outlets to remove the moisture.

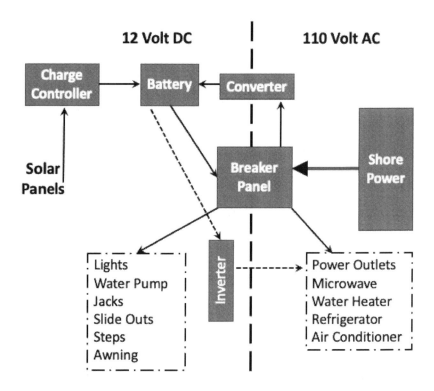

This graphic provides a typical layout of major components and appliances. It may be useful when troubleshooting power related problems keeping in mind that DC failures are related to the battery or Converter whereas other problems are usually traced back to shore power.

Without some electrical background, most people find RV electrical systems to be intimidating and hard to understand. And no doubt most owners will be flying blind for the first few months until things start to click in. And therefore I stress the need to learn how the battery is charged and have a plan to keep it charged to prevent premature battery failure and to save you money. It is not all that critical you know how to operate the Inverter or to know much about it at first. But it is critical to keep your battery heathy and ready to go when you need it.

The Q&A and Troubleshooting Guide in the Appendix has many scenarios on electrical failures and how to isolate the cause and perform common corrective actions. Just remember how this chapter started by splitting the electrical system into a DC system and AC system. When something fails the quickest way to get it restored is to determine if it is DC or AC powered. DC failures almost ALWAYS relate back to the battery or converter whereas AC failures are shore power or breaker panel issues.

Pro Tip: Modern electronics are susceptible to damage from high and low voltages as well as various grounding issues. To protect your RV, get a good Electrical Management System and not just a Surge Protector. I recommend Progressive Industries EMS.

Notes:

Appliances

We need our appliances to ensure we have the basic comforts of home however RV appliances are quite different from what we typically have at home. RV appliances require a basic understanding of how they are powered and how to troubleshoot issues and symptoms when a problem arises. We will look at each appliance, how they are powered, typical problems and required maintenance.

12 Volt Direct Current	110 Volt Alternating Current	LP
Lights	Microwave	Stove Top
Fans	Refrigerator	Refrigerator
Furnace	Air Conditioner	Furnace
Thermostat	Water Heater (Option)	Hot Water (Option)
Hydraulics (Jacks/Slides)	TV – Sound System	Generator
Inverter (power source)	Electrical Outlets	Oven

Stovetop/Range

Usually a simple 2, 3 or 4 burner propane stovetops with electronic spark device. The propane or liquid propane (LP) is used as fuel. To verify the LP system and to confirm the LP tanks have fuel you can light the stovetop.

Conventional Oven

This is a propane burner oven with temperature control. Usually, a pilot light must be lit before the oven will operate. Some of the newer units will have an electronic starter.

> **Pro Tip:** If a propane appliance will not operate turn off the tank valves and reopen very slowly. Place a stovetop burner to the Light Position allowing all air to exit the system and continue to ignite until a flame is achieved.

Hot Water Heater

Most Hot Water Heaters usually have Gas and Electric modes. The gas mode heats fastest. However, the electric will use the campgrounds electrical power which is free. I recommend turning the water heater off when not in use regardless of which mode you use.

Typical RV dual mode hot water heaters are manufactured by either Suburban or Atwood. Suburban water heater tanks are porcelain-lined steel and require an anode rod to prevent corrosion of the steel tank. Atwood water heaters have an aluminum tank and do not require an anode rod. The anode rod should be inspected and replaced every 18 to 24 months. Replacement rods are inexpensive and can be obtained from most home improvement stores.

To reduce the amount of wasted water while waiting for the water to get warm, many newer units have tankless water heaters. Tankless heaters are propane operated devices which heat the water immediately when the hot water faucet is opened. These tankless heaters are sensitive to water pressure which is the key to activating the heater. The heaters can be problematic with fluctuating water pressure.

Furnace

Propane furnace with a thermostat, usually the same thermostat as the air conditioner. The furnace has an external exhaust on the outside of your RV which should be kept clean. A common problem is spider webs or wasp nests in the burner assembly. Use compressed air or if not available a vacuum cleaner can clear the spider webs.

Although the furnace operates on propane it requires 12v DC to run the blower or fan. When boondocking in cold weather the furnace blower can consume a large amount of battery power and should be monitored closely to prevent over discharging the batteries.

Microwave or Micro Convection Oven

The microwave in the RV may be remarkably similar to a small microwave you would find in a home. Shore power will be necessary for operation. A quick way to determine if your RV has shore power is to check the clock on the microwave; no clock means no shore power. A typical problem of operating the microwave is overloading the 30-amp RV electrical system. In this case you may need to turn off other high amperage electrical devices such as air conditioners, hot water heater, space heaters and hair dryers when using the microwave. 50-amp RV system should not experience this condition.

Air Conditioner

This is what I consider essential camping equipment in the South where I live, and I even highly recommend two air conditioners if within your budget and available on your RV configuration. Operation is like a residential air conditioner, controlled by a thermostat. Of course, 30-amp or 50-amp shore power (or generator) is required and in some cases the thermostat is powered by 12v DC power (Furnace also).

RV models with 2 or more air conditioners are configured for 50-amp electrical service. This allows 2 AC units to operate at the same time and continue to supply other electrical devices with needed amperage.

An important consideration when shopping for an RV is the distribution of air flow and air conditioner noise. Ducked air conditioning is becoming more popular which delivers cool air more evenly distributed throughout the RV. The ducted system operates with much less noise.

Air conditioners require a minimum 30-amp power connection to operate properly. Using a 15-amp or 20-amp connection from your home may operate the unit but it will damage the internal air conditioner components.

Refrigerator

You may have an electric/LP, 12v only, or residential refrigerator. The most common is the electric/LP which automatically switches mode based on what is available. The residential is 110v only and operates from the inverter. The 12v only uses the RV battery.

A few RV electric/LP refrigerators have been reported to be problematic due to hot air venting issues. A common solution is to add small 12v fans in the outside refrigerator compartment forcing the air up and out of the roof vent. I'm not sure what specific makes or year models are affected however, I have seen it on several different fifth wheels with kitchen slides. Again, this only affected a small number of RV configurations and those design issues have been resolved on newer models.

Residential refrigerators work exceptionally well and can be quite large with some even having ice makers. They usually require a 1000-watt pure sine wave inverter with power outlets wired for shore power and inverter power. When on shore power the inverter can be turned off.

Each appliance has a manufacturer's warranty, and some offer an extended warranty for a fee or sometimes free with product registration. It is also a good idea to complete the product registration forms so you will be notified of any future recall notices.

Pro Tip: Flashing clock on the microwave is the quickest way to verify you have 110v power. When troubleshooting LP problems always ensure the rangetop will light first. Turn on the refrigerator 24 to 48 hours before departing on a trip to ensure it has sufficient time to cool.

Refer to the Troubleshooting Guide for specifics on common appliance failures and solutions.

Notes:

Tires and Batteries

What is going to cost you money when you least expect it? You got it, tires and batteries. We don't like these kinds of surprises especially when most of us take for granted the tires and batteries will last for years and we just don't need to worry about them.

A certain amount of RV owner expense will be in tires and batteries which could average out to several hundred dollars per year. Granted these expenses will be small regarding to total operating expenses such as fuel, campground fees or periodic maintenance especially on diesel engine vehicles. However, these are expenses that most owners don't plan for until a problem or emergency occurs.

Unbelievable, but true, the underlying cause for a large percentage of tire and battery failures are due to the RV owner's negligence. In other words, wasted money that could have been spent camping in Key West. Let's address each of these and outline what you as an RV owner can do to minimize these expenses.

Tires

Another astonishing fact is that too many RV manufactures use "budget tires" as standard equipment when much better alternatives are available at a higher cost point. This shifts the burden to you in determining what specific tire you have and what is the performance track record of that tire.

We have all heard the term "China Bomb" but who knows exactly what brand or brands fall into this category? I strongly believe that any tire can become a bomb if not properly maintained. The overwhelming cause of blowouts or premature tire failure is running the tire with insufficient air pressure. Therefore, you must learn the correct air pressure for your tires relative to the weight of your RV. Check the air pressure when the tires are cold (have not been driven) every travel day. This means every morning you intend to drive, check the tire pressure, and set each tire to the correct psi. This will greatly extend the life of you tires and may prevent damage to your RV or injury to you and your family.

Pro Tip: Use a good Tire Pressure Monitoring System (TPMS) to ensure you always have the correct air pressure. The system will monitor air pressure and tire temperature while traveling and provide a warning should the pressure or temperature reach dangerous levels.

RV tires are subject to ultraviolet (UV) light damage and should be covered when in storage or between trips. Old age and NOT tread depth will determine when to replace your tires. Depending on operating and storage conditions RV tires should be replaced every 4 to 6 years regardless of how good they may look.

Battery

Almost every day I read where an RV owner is reporting dead batteries on a new RV and they can't understand why. And the sad thing is that in most cases the dead batteries are not a warranty covered failure costing the RV owner hundreds of dollars to replace. In many of these cases the failure could have been prevented if properly maintained. Let's take this opportunity now to better understand the battery, how to keep the battery happy and how to keep money in your pocket.

Batteries are nothing more than a storage device to hold 12v DC power for distribution and use throughout your RV. As we learned in a previous chapter, the purpose of the converter is to keep the battery charged when connected to shore or generator power. A quick note here, solar panels charge the battery directly using a solar charge controller and do not require or use the converter.

When considering lead acid batteries, a healthy battery is a fully charged battery. Allowing your battery to sit in an uncharged state will reduce its service life. When a battery is not allowed to fully charge sulfation occurs. Sulfation will cause crystals to form on the battery plates not allowing the battery to accept a complete charge thusly the battery capacity is reduced.

Additionally, allowing a battery to discharge below 50 percent capacity will cause sulfation. Repeated over-discharging will result in premature battery failure requiring battery replacement.

Charge	12 Volt
100%	12.73
90%	12.62
80%	12.5
70%	12.37
60%	12.24
50%	12.10
40%	11.96
30%	11.81
20%	11.66
10%	11.51

The state of battery charge is displayed in this chart. The battery must be at rest and not being used when the voltage reading is taken. As a good rule to protect your battery never discharge below 60 per cent and monitor the battery voltage closely when dry camping or camping without electrical service.

Most recreational vehicles have a Battery Disconnect switch which isolates the battery from the electrical system and attempts to prevent the battery from discharging. Even with this switch engaged there is always a small power drain on the battery such as CO_2 and Propane Detectors, entertainment systems with a clock or internal memory and possibly other devices. My experience is that the Battery Disconnect may protect your battery for just a few days, but any period longer will result in a dead battery condition. An especially important point is with the Battery Disconnect engaged the converter will not charge the battery. Some manufactures are starting to wire the converter differently, but it has not yet become an industry standard at this point.

Pro Tip: Whenever possible keep your RV connected to shore power, even if that means using a power adapter to connect 110v from you home. Other methods include using a solar battery charger or moving the batteries to a location with power and place them on a multi-stage smart charger. Use a quality charger and not a cheap trickle charger which may damage your battery over time.

Notes on My Tires

Brand: _____

Style/Model: _____

Size: _____

Air Pressure: _____ psi

Date of Manufacture: _____

Notes on My Battery

Brand: _____

Group: _____

Type: _____ (Flooded, Gel, AGM, Lithium)

Amp Hour Rating: _____

Date of Install: _____

Jack Hunnicutt

Part IV

To conquer frustration, one must remain intensely focused on the outcome, not the obstacles.

~TF Hodge

Arizona - New Mexico State Line - Interstate 10

Roadside Assistance

It is always a great plan to have a good roadside assistance policy in place when you travel with an RV. These programs provide a wide range of services but what will most likely affect your travel is towing, tire failure, dead battery, and lockout.

There is a long list of roadside service providers and some providers are better than others while a few are just not worth considering. Check first with your insurance company to determine if an "RV Plan" is available and make sure you emphasize RV because auto plans do not cover recreational vehicles. I have read many reviews on roadside assistance providers and one common issue is that in your time of need some providers will just not cover the situation for various reasons. Read the small print and ask questions and most importantly ask other RV owners for recommendations. And when evaluating different plans keep in mind that the cheaper plans will usually buy you less service.

Some providers like AAA do not cover RVs unless you upgrade to their AAA Premium Plan. Coach-Net is an RV only business and specializes in the RV Industry. Others may offer coverage for a small initial price that could increase significantly in later years. Whatever you do don't go cheap because chances are you will get less service on your next emergency.

Towing

A good Roadside Assistance plan will offer RV towing to the nearest authorized service center. Some providers will only allow a specific number of miles for the tow such as within 50 miles. The plan should include the tow vehicle and the trailer. Therefore, it is important to rigorously evaluate plans offered by automobile insurance companies to ensure the proper coverage for recreational vehicles.

Tire Failures

RV tires can be difficult to change especially with motorhomes and larger trailers. The tire service will include changing the tire but not damage repair or tire replacement. In the case of motorhomes without spare tires, the provider will locate a compatible tire at a cost to you and mount the new tire on the motorhome.

Dead Battery

There can be many reasons why a battery drains down or goes bad and it usually happens at the worst times, especially in cold weather. Be proactive and carry jumper cables or an electrical power boost. Roadside Assistance will provide a jump if needed. Any additional service to replace or charge the battery will result in an extra charge.

Lockout

We never expect this to happen, but it does happen all too often. The lock out service will get you back into the RV or vehicle but depending on your location it may be an extended wait for the provider to arrive. This is yet another reason to keep an extra set of keys in a safe location outside of the RV.

> **Pro Tip:** There is nothing that can spoil a camping trip faster than a flat tire. Obtain a good heavy-duty tire pressure gauge and air compressor. When in areas with poor or no cell phone service you may have to change a tire even if you have a roadside assistance policy.

Notes:

Security

Insurance is the best way to protect the investment you have in your RV and in most, if not all states Liability insurance is mandatory. Banks, Credit Unions, and other lenders require Comprehensive and Collision insurance to protect their collateral on the RV loan. This is mostly common knowledge, but I wanted to cover a slightly different aspect of security and that is the pro-active steps you can take to secure your investment.

Recreational vehicle theft is a real problem and deserves your attention. There are measures you can take to be pro-active to reduce your chances of becoming a victim. Motorhomes, travel trailers and fifth wheels are quite different in the measures you can take to make them secure. Anything from hitch coupler locks, king pin locks, electronic door locks, wheel boots, and full-blown security systems.

No lock is infallible, just take a look at YouTube and you will find videos showing how to defeat almost any locking device you can purchase. A little scary isn't it? The reason we put our faith in locks is to give us a certain level of comfort knowing that at a minimum the average person will not have access to your valuables and the lock may slow down if not prevent the professional thieves.

Here are some tips to use in addition to the security devices mentioned.

- Never leave an RV on the side of the road, stay with the vehicle until help arrives
- Use the door's deadbolt if available, door latch locks may use common key sets
- Be aware of your surroundings and don't leave an RV in public areas (outside of a campground) for extended periods
- Tracking devices may get your RV back if stolen but, in many cases the RV will be damaged or trashed and you may not want it back
- Review your insurance and roadside assistance program annually

.

If you don't already know, I'll break the cold hard facts to you, some RVs have the same lock/key combinations. RV door and storage compartment locking keys in many cases are matched sets over and over meaning that other campers nearby may have a key that fits your storage compartments and possibly your entrance door. This is one reason I recommend if you have a deadbolt lock installed that is what you should use. Deadbolts are less likely to be duplicated and in some rare cases no duplications at all. Other options are Electronic or Keypad locking systems which are available as replacements for many RV door locks. Replacement storage compartment locks are available online at Amazon or a local locksmith or home improvement store.

Hitch and hitch coupler locks can significantly decrease the chances of your RV or hitch from being stolen. Choose a coupler lock that has a good history and high recommendation from fellow RV owners and RV professionals. One that I recommend is the Proven Locks coupler lock which is constructed of quarter-inch steel. There are many good hitch pin locking devices that will keep your hitch safe.

For fifth wheels (travel trailers too) a wheel boot is an excellent way to prevent the trailer from being towed away. You may also want to disable electronic/hydraulic jacks and stabilizer by removing associated fuses. Fifth wheel hitches are rarely subject to thief purely because of their weight however, I would recommend a truck bed cover to keep it out of sight.

> **Pro Tip:** To prevent a lock out situation keep a spare set of main entrance door keys in a safe location outside of your RV. I won't recommend any specific locations here due to security concerns but obtain a magnetic key holder and be creative in finding a safe place to keep your spare keys.

Your RV is your home, at least while you are on the road so take the necessary steps to stay secure. Remember that cheap locks are cheap for a reason--inferior materials and poor design. When you don't have a good feeling about a particular campground or boondocking site put it in Drive and leave. Instincts are right more than we think. Finally, don't let friends or family borrow your RV, it will never come back the same, but this is a whole different issue.

In summary, be proactive when it comes to securing your RV. A stolen RV in most cases will eventually be returned to its owner but hardly ever in good operating condition. It may be damaged and trashed out or even something worse. Therefore, I'm not a big fan of tracking devices instead I like putting my money in the actual preventative steps and not in the recovery of a stolen RV.

Notes:

Safety

Have you noticed all the safety stickers on your RV? Sometimes we may feel that safety concerns are overstated, and just maybe common sense should suffice and I agree completely. However, I'm sure there are many legal considerations that motivate the need and placement of these stickers. I don't want you to ignore that information, but I do want to include some additional safety considerations.

Driving safety is addressed in other chapters and not repeated here. Refer to Part V, The Journey, for information on daily driving and the Ready to Drive checklist.

This guidance on safety generally applies to all travel trailers, fifth wheels and motorhomes however, you should become familiar with the specific guidance for your RV which is provided in owner's manuals and other RV documentation.

Outside

The hitch coupler on travel trailers is designed to connect to the hitch ball on your tow vehicle and if you look closely you will see a hole going through the coupler latch. This is a safety design to accommodate a latch pin that will prevent the coupler latch from inadvertently opening and potentially coming off the hitch ball. I would not recommend using a lock instead of the pin because in case of a trailer fire it will be more difficult to unhook the tow vehicle and move it away from the fire.

The liquid propane (LP) tanks are secured to prevent the tanks from moving or becoming dislodged when traveling. Periodically check to ensure the tanks are secure and will not move. Some people want to use a locking device to secure the tanks and this is a personal preference. I believe locks are not necessary unless you are parking in a very crime prone area.

The LP tanks can be left in the open position to allow for use when camping and it is also acceptable to operate the refrigerator on LP when travelling except in restricted areas such as tunnels and some bridges. Show your co-pilot and older children how to turn off the tanks in the event of an emergency such as a LP leak.

Periodically check the LP feed lines, especially around the bottom of the tanks where the tank cover sits on the frame (on trailers). Look for any chaffing or damage to the lines and have any damage repaired immediately. Look at the LP quick disconnect port (if equipped) to ensure it has not become damaged by rocks and road debris. You can use a spray bottle of soapy water to spray on lines and fittings to identify any leaks by watching for bubbles.

Tires and trailer brakes must be functioning properly before departing on any trip, long or short. *Refer to Part III, Tires and Battery, for specifics on inspecting tires. Part I, Conducting the PDI, discusses setting the brake controller.* Motorhome brakes should be inspected and maintained as described in your vehicle owner's manual.

Use wheel chocks to secure your RV from unexpected movement and rolling. It is important to do this immediately upon leveling and setting the stabilizers/jacks. Frequently stabilizers are damaged when the RV shifts or moves causing the stabilizers to bend. More serious damage and injury can occur if chocks are not used to secure the unit from rolling. Even if X-Chocks are used you still need to place wheel chocks on both sides of at least one wheel.

The entrance steps can create a hazard if not deployed properly or if they become slippery from mud, water, or some other substance. At first the trailer steps may be a little tricky to fold out and make secure.

For obvious reasons, the hot water heater and furnace discharge hot air when operating on LP. The exhaust vents can become extremely hot when in operation creating a burn hazard to people and objects. It is a good practice to NOT place outside furniture or other items in front of these vents.

Inside

All adults and older children should be aware of the location and operation of the fire extinguisher. In addition to the entrance door, there is at least one emergency exit from your RV. This is usually a window in the bedroom area that is designed for quick opening in case of an emergency. You may also have a second door or hatch that can be used as an exit. I recommend conducting an exercise to keep everyone familiar with how to exit the RV under emergency circumstances.

Your RV will have a Smoke Detector and LP Detector. Each of these can be tested periodically by following the instructions on the unit. They are powered by 12v DC power and may need replacing after several years of operation. Refer to the actual device for specific details on replacement.

I recommend keeping a small First Aid Kit in your RV. This would include medical coverings and treatments for injuries at the campsite or on the hiking trail. Also include insect repellent and treatments for insect bites and other skin related issues such as poison ivy, poison oak and fire ant bites.

When traveling, items inside cabinets can shift and lodge against the doors waiting to fall once the door is opened. This happened to us on one of our first trips causing several Corning Ware plates to fall and break into hundreds of sharp pieces. Be incredibly careful when opening cabinets after travel and you may also want to use only unbreakable dinner ware.

And finally, a precaution that you may view differently. I do not recommend using candles in any recreational vehicle. Of course, your stovetop has an open flame, but it is much less likely to cause a fire than a candle which can easily be overturned or pushed against a cushion or curtain. As an alternative, you may want to investigate using electronic candles. They offer some of the same ambience as burning candles and may also add a fragrance while providing safety in your RV.

Please read, understand, and follow the safety/warning stickers on your RV and don't forget to read the owner's manual and other documentation provided for appliances.

Notes:

Jack Hunnicutt

Part V

Life is an adventure, it's not a package tour.
~Eckhart Tolle

Route 66 - Winslow, Arizona

Trip Planning

As with real estate, camping is also about location, location, location. Hopefully, you live in a region of our great nation that offers camping opportunities nearby. Campgrounds within close driving distances are great for shakedown trips to allow you and your RV an opportunity for some break-in camping experiences. And who knows, you may like the local places so much they may become your favorites.

In any case some level of planning is necessary to optimize your time and money for quality camping and traveling adventures. Besides, it is all about fun, so you want everything to be as worry-free as possible. Reservations can and will take a lot of stress out of your traveling by just knowing you have a safe place to park and camp at the end of the day. In most "destination" locations reservations are a must and when visiting popular areas or attractions this means making plans and reservations months in advance. National Parks, many state parks, and any campground along the coast or scenic locations in the mountains require reservations.

Phone Apps & Internet Planning Tools

If you are not Internet savvy you will have difficulty with planning since online is the preferred method for checking availability and making reservations. But the good news is there are numerous websites and apps available that can simplify the process.

A short list of available smartphone apps and resources include RV Parking, Campground Reviews, Allstays Camp & RV, Allstays C-RV Military, Reserve America, Recreation.gov, The Dyrt Tent & RV, Campendium RV & Tent, USFS & BLM Campgrounds, and Campground Review/RV Trip Wizard by RV Life.

Online reviews and word of mouth are essential in picking campgrounds that will meet your expectations. Web Forums and Facebook Groups are a great starting place to tap into the experience of your fellow RV owners. When considering campgrounds ensure they have hookups, activities, and other amenities you require in addition to shopping opportunities for stocking up on food, supplies and fuel.

Reservations Required

The days of rolling up to a popular campground and asking for campsite are in our rearview mirrors. As the RV community continues to grow, campground availability becomes more of a premium often requiring reservations. The more popular destination campgrounds may require reservations 6 to 12 months in advance. This includes areas within and around major national parks such as Yellowstone, Glacier, Grand Canyon, Bryce Canyon and Grand Tetons to name a few. This is also becoming the new normal at most state parks and private campgrounds in popular locations.

The RV industry in general is either a feast or famine situation and with current RV sales breaking records you would think new recreational investments would be looking at opportunities for new campgrounds and RV resorts. I'm just not seeing many new camping facilities opening to satisfy the current void. But I do see Buc-ee's mega fuel stations spreading into states outside of Texas, meaning recreational travel is on the rise and just maybe there is a rebirth of new camping locations over the horizon.

> **Pro Tip:** Be proficient in using phone apps to locate campgrounds while traveling. You will not always have reservations. Many State Parks offer walkup campsite assignments on a first come first serve basis. Municipal and county campgrounds are usually well-kept secrets but can be gems. I use RV Trip Wizard which I will cover in the next chapter.

Clubs, Parks, Memberships and Subscriptions

In other words, it's time to discuss some of the available resources that are pay as you go. The free smartphone apps and websites previously mentioned may be all you need, and many people lock on to one or two campground locating apps and they are happy campers. But the RV world offers much more variety at a nominal expense should you want to maximize your opportunities.

Clubs

There are virtually hundreds of Clubs with local and national chapters which often are free to join or requiring a $10 to $30 annual club fee. Almost every RV major manufacturer (Thor, Forest River, Keystone, Winnebago the top four) have clubs and many have additional clubs for individual brands such as Montana, Cedar Creek, Bigfoot, Lance, Cougar and Jayco just to name a few. These clubs may be a good fit if you like meeting and camping with owners of your same RV brand or model. Most have periodic and annual rallies.

National & State Parks

Each state park system has different policies on discounts, fees and annual or seasonal passes. Many will offer senior, permanent disability or veteran discounts while some require proof of state residency to qualify for discounts. Call ahead or check their website for specific discount information.

The National Park's America the Beautiful Passes have some of the best discounts or free access programs of all that are offered across the country. Since National Parks are an extremely popular camping, hiking and sightseeing destination, it will be to your advantageous for you to investigate which programs you may be eligible.

Annual Pass: Currently available for $80 and may be obtained at any federal recreation site, by phone or online. Check the nps.gov website for details.

Military Pass: This is a free annual pass available to Current U.S. military members and their dependents in the Army, Navy, Air Force, Marines, Coast Guard, and Space Force, as well as Reserve and National Guard members. The pass may be obtained in person at a federal recreation site by showing a Common Access Card (CAC) or Military ID (Form 1173).

Veterans and Gold Star Families: Beginning on Veterans Day, November 11, 2020, Gold Star Families and U.S. military veterans receive free access to more than 2,000 federal recreation areas, including national parks, wildlife refuges, and forests. A veteran is identified as an individual who has served in the U.S. Armed Forces, including the National Guard and Reserves, and is able to present one of the following forms of identification when entering a national park:
- Department of Defense Identification Card (CAC Card)
- Veteran Health Identification Card (VHIC)
- Veteran ID Card
- Veterans designation on a state-issued U.S. driver's license or identification card

Senior Pass: Available to U.S. citizens or permanent residents age 62 or over. Applicants must provide documentation of age and residency or citizenship. A one-time fee of $80 or a yearly fee of $20.

Access Pass: A free lifetime pass for U.S. citizens or permanent residents with permanent disabilities. Applicants must provide documentation of permanent disability and residency or citizenship.

Pro Tip: Senior Pass and Access Pass may provide a 50 percent discount on some amenity fees charged for facilities and services such as camping, swimming, boat launch, and specialized interpretive services.

Memberships

Discount memberships require an annual fee in exchange for discounts at participating campgrounds. The fees and discounts vary significantly among the different programs. Two popular memberships are Good Sam Club and Passport America. Camping five to ten nights per year utilizing either of these programs can save the price of annual membership.

The Harvest Host annual membership offers free overnight camping at a network of host locations at wineries, breweries, museums, farms, dairies and more. This is dry camping without hookups. Making a courtesy purchase from the host is recommended.

Boondockers Welcome has the most diverse setting for camping than other programs. This is also an annual membership to access their network of host locations for free overnight camping and in many locations multi-night camping is offered. The locations range from rural, urban and remote and don't be surprised to even find driveway camping. Again, it is recommended that you provide the host with an inexpensive gift or a small complementary payment.

Subscriptions

Subscriptions which either allow access to a product or campgrounds are becoming more widely accepted.

RV Trip Wizard is an online subscription-based planning tool which creates routes and displays campgrounds, attractions, food, fuel, rest areas and much more along the way. An all-in-one package to organize the entire trip which is also integrated with a smartphone app to use while traveling. The app has all the planning details and a RV Friendly GPS showing bridge and tunnel clearance, elevation and grade driving hazards.

There are other programs that involve a long-term or multi-year commitment such as Thousand Trails and Coast to Coast RV Resorts and Campgrounds. They also offer member privileges at campground networks across the United States at differ levels of membership.

Pro Tip: In addition to memberships listed here, many campgrounds will offer discounts to Seniors, Military, First Responders, and other groups like AAA, FMCA, AARP and National Park's America the Beautiful Access Pass and Senior Pass.

As with any discount program read the fine print and understand all the terms and conditions before joining. You will find that in some programs the discounts may require cash only transactions, additional charges for 3 or more people in an RV and limits on the number of days you may reserve or stay at the campground. Don't be shy or afraid to ask for a discount every time you register at a campground or make reservations.

Notes:

The Journey

Whether you know it or not you have two new best friends; the GPS and your side-view mirrors. One is for going forward the other looking at where you have been, but both are essential, and both will keep you out of trouble.

Properly adjusted mirrors will provide a complete picture of your RV allowing you to drive with confidence and safety. If your mirror includes a blind-spot mirror (small section providing wide angle view) you will be able to view your motorhome or trailer wheels as you make cornering turns.

There are many good options for RV GPS solutions. Ensure the GPS considers the dimensions, especially the height, of your RV when preparing routes to avoid hazards such as low bridges, tunnels, and narrow mountain roads. Many vehicles come standard with GPS units which may be sufficient. However, I recommend using a map (hardcopy or online) to conduct a dry run of the route to verify routing, tunnels, bridges etc.

Daily Driving

The distance you travel each day depends on many factors including driving speed. A RV driving instructor trained me to drive at 63 MPH which allows the faster traffic to swing around you and get out of the way. This will significantly minimize the number of traffic lane changes you make. As it turns out this works great for my tow vehicle, best MPG, and favorable operating temperatures for the engine and transmission.

If your destination is only a few hundred miles away or closer, you can complete the journey easily in one day. However, for longer multi-day trips the distance you travel each day will depend on road and weather conditions, driving experience, family and pet needs, planned and unplanned stops for rest and sightseeing. Synchronizing your trip to arrive at attractions and "destination" campgrounds at just the right time can be a little tricky but with some detailed planning you can do it and it does get easier with time.

Weather Concerns

Always consider weather conditions regardless of the time of year. The mid-west in Spring is tornado season, June through November in the South is hurricane season and of course winter presents challenges depending on your specific location. Aside from these mentioned weather conditions blowing winds pose a profoundly serious situation for RV travel.

Your RV is a large object traveling at highway speeds and can easily be affected by wind. Each RV will be a little different but winds above 20 MPH can be dangerous. Be willing to accept the fact that you may have to get off the road and give the conditions a chance to improve. Don't push yourself to make any specific destination or milestone; be safe first and always. Spending the night in a Walmart parking lot makes more sense than gambling with you RV or your family's safety.

> **Pro Tip:** Always give yourself sufficient driving time and avoid having to drive long hours just to make a reservation. Know how many hours per day you will drive and stick to it. Have a plan to be at your campground between 4 PM and 6 PM each day. Arriving after dark should be avoided.

Establish a Routine

Establish a routine to follow when driving. Many of us have the dash cluttered with gadgets, wires, maps and who knows what else which can quickly become a distraction and a possible safety issue. Maintain some reasonable level of organization so that when you need something you don't have to go looking for it. For example, who has ever heard an annoying beeping sound and couldn't determine if it were the TPMS, GPS, Radio, Vehicle Alert, or the kid's toys in the back seat? Driving at highway speeds is not a good time to join the scavenger hunt to find the beeping sound.

Work with your Co-pilot and develop your own driving process. It's best to write it down so you are both working off the same page (no pun intended). After the first few trips evaluate how the driving experience went and modify your process as needed. Here are a few recommendations that may help get you started.

Ready to Drive?

- Don't drive until everything is ready including passengers, pets, and vehicle
- Outside walk around complete (check tow/hitch setup, all obstacles removed)
- Double check to ensure all hoses, electrical connections and wheel chocks removed
- Inspect tires for road damage, bulges, cracks, or signs of tread separation
- Check lights (brake, turn signals, driving and daytime running lights)
- GPS set for the next destination or Co-pilot is prepared to assist with navigation
- Vehicle is in tow/haul mode if necessary and exhaust brake engaged if available
- Tire Pressure Monitoring System active, tires properly inflated and monitor within view
- Mirrors properly adjusted

Periodic Road Checks

- Stop at the "first" rest area or pull off the road and perform a walk around check
- Tow/hitch setup good, all safety pins in place
- Feel tires and wheel hubs for excessive heat
- Inspect tires for road damage, bulges, cracks, or signs of tread separation
- Look for open RV windows or doors (doors should be locked)
- Storage compartments closed
- Plan to do this again at next fuel stop

Driving Tips

The actual task of driving or towing your new RV will begin with major episodes of stress and anxiety which subsides quickly with experience. If an RV driving class is available, I recommend both Pilot and Co-Pilot take the course. There are some valuable lessons to be learned in a good driving class that will make the driving experience safer and much more enjoyable.

In a previous chapter we discussed driving and backing in the campground all of which is low speed maneuvering. Driving at higher speeds isn't much different with a few exceptions. First you need to stay focused in front well ahead of your vehicle and this will help you line up for driving in your lane and staying straight. If you start looking at the tips of your fenders you will lose perception and start to sway. This really comes in to play when driving in constructions zones with no road shoulder and driving close to the ever-present orange barrels. Just keep looking ahead with an occasional glance in the side mirrors and you will remain straight.

Turning will come much easier with practice. Make necessary adjustments for wide turns to allow your trailer ample space to clear traffic and curbing. The trailer will turn sharper than the tow vehicle and requires the tow vehicle to make a wide sweeping turn to give the trailer enough space. As mentioned earlier, you can use the blind spot mirror to watch the trailer wheel clear the side curb. With motorhomes turning is a little different and easier. I have found it helpful to wait until your hip (yes, your actual hip) is aligned with the turn before turning the wheel. This should give you sufficient clearance for the turn. Also, if your motorhome is pulling a TOAD it will track almost exactly in the wheel path of the motorhome.

Getting Fuel

No matter how hard you try to avoid fuel stations, sooner or later you must refuel. Here I go again with my proactive sermon but plan and know approximately if not exactly where you will refuel. There are many smartphone apps like Gas Buddy that can assist in locating stations, but the key is not just locating a station but locating a station where you can safely get in and get out.

Truck stops are almost a sure thing for having pump placements allowing larger vehicles. Some truck stops including Flying J offer RV only gasoline and diesel fuel pumps with plenty of space to maneuver. If you have a diesel vehicle you can use the same pumps as the large trucks, but you must learn the rules of pulling ahead to allow the next vehicle in line access to the pump while you go inside to make purchases or use the restroom.

I am definitely a Journey person and I like the travel aspect just as much as the destination. We all have made a significant investment in our RV and we should take pride in not only how it looks but how it performs on the road. As the driver/operator you are unquestionably the most essential component to a safe and enjoyable trip so rise to the challenge and I know you will.

Pro Tip: Train yourself to be thinking ahead. Your RV is not designed to make quick turns or U-turns like an automobile. You need to be thinking about the route ahead to prevent any sudden changes to navigation. I like to keep at least the next 2 or 3 turns in my head even when driving with a GPS. This gives you a chance to consider low clearance bridges and tunnels, prepare for extreme angle turns like something greater than 90 degrees, and of course it gives you time to get in the proper lane for making a turn.

Notes:

Boondocking, Dry Camping and Free Parking

All these terms are remarkably close yet different in definition, but they have one thing in common: *camping without any hook ups.* No electric, no water, no sewer and in many cases no bathhouse or rest room. Your RV really needs to be self-contained which means it provides all the services you require.

This type of camping can take place in many different settings, anything from National Parks, Bureau of Land Management (BLM) property, Walmart, or Cracker Barrel parking lots or even in someone's driveway, pasture, or farmland. Some are free while other locations may have a camping fee. Additionally, there are membership-based programs such as Harvest Host and Boondockers Welcome which offer nationwide camping opportunities.

Boondocking and Dry Camping

You may be looking for a quick free spot for an overnight stop to rest before traveling on which may be one of the parking lot options. This "courtesy" parking should always be at the approval of the property owner or manager and remember it is a free place to park and not a place to setup you grill and get out the lounge chairs.

On the other hand, some folks head off to the wilderness and enjoy the remote spaces of BLM and other public land camping. Again, there are rules and, in some cases, permits and fees are required. Do your homework and try to find someone that can show you the ropes before you go.

Managing your resources is essential regarding water, electricity, and wastewater disposal. Solar or generator power is necessary to keep the RV batteries charged. Conserving water usage is necessary to extend the availability of fresh water in your tank and to minimize the amount of wastewater produced. A portable wastewater tank is typically used to transport the gray water to a dump station. I don't recommend transporting black water in a portable tank for sanitation concerns, yet some campers do endorse this practice.

Of course, for just an overnight stop the only real concern is not running down the batteries. The major power usage will be the refrigerator which requires DC power (residential refrigerator will use the battery connected inverter) and the minimal amount of lighting you will need.

Free Parking

Overnight parking at Walmart has been taken for granted by many and frequently abused by a few. Each Walmart has different policies and local laws and ordinances to follow. Call ahead and ask if they allow overnight parking. Usually anyone that answers the phone will be knowledgeable and can answer your questions but if necessary, go inside the store and speak with the on-duty manager. They will usually ask that you depart by a specific time and to park in a designated section of the parking lot. It is customary to do some shopping as a courtesy.

Cracker Barrel restaurants frequently have larger parking areas for overnight RV parking. Again, you should check with the management to ensure you are welcomed to stay. And the next morning enjoy a hot breakfast and let them know you appreciate their hospitality.

Other locations to check for free overnight parking are Cabela's who offer free dump sites and water at some locations. Truck stops such as Flying J and Pilot may also permit overnight parking in designated RV parking spaces separate from the semi-tractor trailer parking. My experience is that truck stops can be very safe since they are well-lighted and always have people present. The downside to truck stops is the noise, big trucks seem to never shutdown their engines and they make a lot of noise. But if you want a midnight snack or cup of coffee you can't beat a truck stop.

> **Pro Tip:** Give boondocking a try, I think it will be fun especially for the kids. There is just something about camping for

free which gives you a good feeling about being an RV owner. And besides, you may wakeup to a great Cracker Barrel breakfast.

Free parking always comes with a price, in the case of Harvest Host and Boondockers Welcome, there is an annual membership fee. For Walmart, Cracker Barrel, and others the price is just to be respectful of their rules, pick up all your trash and remember that it is only overnight parking not camping.

Notes:

Part VI

Positive thinking must be followed by positive doing.
~John C. Maxwell

"Glory" the Airstream at Home

Storing Your RV

For many of us there will come the day that camping is over for the year and it is time to put the RV to "sleep" until next season. Storage is such a sad word to use when referring to what has become our best friend or even a family member, our RV. But by following a few simple steps you ensure everything will remain protected, safe, and ready to hit the road when needed.

Storing indoors or covered by a solid structure is by far preferred over leaving your RV exposed to the elements. In some cases, a soft cover will suffice however there can be issues with moisture buildup and the cover may damage the exterior finish especially on an Airstream's aluminum skin.

Moisture Control

The fight to control and prevent moisture can be a significant effort but worth every penny you spend in prevention. Exposure to the sun will over time cause the exterior caulking and seals on the roof and sides to harden and begin to separate allowing moisture a pathway into your RV. Once inside, moisture can rot the RV from the inside out if not detected and eliminated quickly. Water damage is usually overlooked by the untrained eye so you may want to have an annual inspection by a professional making sure you take appropriate action on all recommended repairs.

Consider running a dehumidifier to control the humidity if shore power is available. You can use products such as Damp-Rid keeping in mind they will only be affective for small, confided spaces like a cabinet or closet and not your entire RV.

Protect the Battery

I think by now we have learned that if a lead acid battery is not kept fully charged it begins to sulfate leading to premature battery failure. When placing your Airstream in storage the battery will fall in to one of the following scenarios.

- Storage facility has power, and the RV can remain plugged in to shore power (at least 110v AC)
- Storage facility has power, and the battery will be placed on a multi-stage smart charger
- Storage facility does not have power, but the RV's solar system can maintain the battery charge
- Storage facility does not have power therefore the batteries will be removed from the RV and taken to a safe place and put on a multi-stage smart charger
- The Lithium batteries will be stored with a 40-60 percent charge (not fully charged) requiring no attention for 6 to 12 months

There may be other scenarios such as using a portable solar charger or maybe you are concerned about lithium battery charging with extremely low temperatures. In the latter case please contact the lithium battery manufacture for specific guidance.

Regarding battery chargers, you will also see them called *trickle chargers* or *battery maintainers*. Whatever the name, use only multi-stage smart chargers to prevent a possibility of over-charging and damage to the battery. One charger can be shared for several batteries by alternating every few weeks.

Rodents, Pests and Weather

Rodent and pest problems can result in significant damage if not prevented or eliminated quickly. Remove all food and seal any access points into the RV. This means getting underneath the RV and using expanding foam, wire mesh or some other material to plug any possible entry points. The home remedy deterrents such as dryer sheet, peppermint oil and such may provide some level of protection, but I'm not yet convinced that anything short eliminating all points of entry is completely effective. I do use the dry sheets and I have two kitty cats on patrol as well; thank you Houdini and Sky Cat.

If storing in a cold climate where temperatures reach freezing or below for an extended number of hours, you will need to winterize your RV. This is a process to remove all of the water from the plumbing lines and holding tanks, then treating with a special RV antifreeze. Do not use automotive antifreeze since it can leave a harmful residue in the freshwater lines and tank which should not be consumed by humans. Refer to your owner's manual for specific instructions on how to winterize or consult with an RV service center who will perform the service for a fee.

The last but clearly not the least important aspect of storage is security. *Refer to the chapter on Security for recommended steps to lock and prevent theft of your RV.* If possible, store in a well-lighted area with a fence and security cameras. If renting from a storage facility, ensure you have read the rental contract and understand the liability considerations.

Pro Tip: Protect your tires by parking on a hard surface such as concrete or asphalt and avoid parking on dirt. Placing thick boards under the tires is also an option. Keep slide outs closed to create the best moisture barrier possible and leave your jacks and stabilizer up, not touching the ground, to minimize rodent entry points. Visit your Airstream frequently if possible, especially before and after any significant weather events.

Notes:

Caring for Your RV

I have owned several recreational vehicles over the years, and have come to learn, that with proper care your RV will continue to look great for many years and will bring a higher resale value. It does take work and a certain amount of diligence to care for your RV properly. Just keep in mind, if the job looks too big break it into sections and spread out the work over several days.

Housekeeping or Interior Cleaning

I say housekeeping because cleaning your RV is much like what you do at home or for full-timers, what you do for a brick-and-mortar home. Frequently I will see a question on "What do I use to clean my toilet?" A brush and a good toilet cleaning product are the correct answers. But I think some people are actually asking about what goes down the toilet that could damage the holding tanks. To avoid possible damage to the tanks, limit the amount of bleach or other harsh chemicals that are flushed down the toilet or drains in the sinks.

Look at your owner's manual for specific guidance on cleaning the interior wall surfaces to avoid scratching or marking the surface. Also, there are different types of floor coverings (solid and woven) with recommended cleaning methods described in the owner's manual. You may want to keep one of the popular brand cordless stick vacuums which do a great job and can be easily stored.

Exterior Cleaning

It is always best to clean the outer surfaces periodically or as needed. I tend to wash before and after each trip. Even while just sitting in covered storage it collects dust and dirt from the air, so I like to wash it before a trip. Upon returning it will have road grime, mud splatter, bird droppings and who knows what else. After one trip I had fresh white caulk splattered all over one rock guard which took a lot of effort to remove.

For some of you who travel full time it may be difficult finding a place to wash your RV. Some but not many campgrounds will allow washing, and some will allow it for a fee. I have used truck washing facilities with great results. These can be hand wash or automated facilities. I prefer the hand washing to avoid any possible damage from the mechanical washing equipment; the automated washing systems such as those for semi-tractor trailers. The strong brushing motion and mechanical arms may damage components on the roof. Typically, you pay by the foot for the length of the RV, but some may have a flat rate.

For the actual washing process, I start at the roof with a very soft brush on an extension rod to clean everything. Then using a clean washing mitt, I go from the front to the rear washing the tires and wheels last.

Caution: While washing the roof, the surface can become very slippery and present a safety hazard. If you are not comfortable (or safe) washing the roof you may want to skip it and let a professional do it at a later time.

For the products I use I like to keep it quite simple ensuring I never use anything that would damage the protective coatings. To wash, I use a name brand wash with added wax such as Turtle Wax. Some manufactures recommend using Dawn Dish Soap on the roof. Dawn does a good job cleaning, but if it drains down the sides of your RV it will remove any wax on the surface. For this reason, I would avoid using this product on the side surfaces.

Decals and graphics require added attention when washing and waxing. Use soft strokes when washing decals and try to avoid putting any pressure on the edges. This is especially important when applying wax. We will learn more about wax and UV protectants in the following paragraphs.

Fiberglass & Metal Exterior

How you maintain the exterior of your RV really depends on how the RV is stored. In the last chapter we learned that covered storage is the preferred method which protects the RV from the natural elements such as water and UV damage. Keep this in mind when considering how frequently you should check caulking and seals.

Recreational vehicles have either a fiberglass or metal exterior. Maintaining the metal panels on an RV is much like on an automobile. Keep the surfaces washed as needed and maintain a coat of wax or other protectant on the metal and follow the manufactures recommendations for best results. The metal surfaces on an Airstream are completely different which I describe in my book, *My Airstream Mentor: How to "Airstream" for Beginners & the Well-Traveled.*

To me fiberglass provides the most beautiful finish however, it is the most difficult to maintain over time. Fiberglass has a gel coat which adds protection and that beautiful shinny finish. As the RV is exposed to the sun, the UV rays will breakdown the outer gel coat allowing the surface to oxidize and become dull. With extreme oxidation the fiberglass will crack. Therefore, it is important to control oxidation before it happens by protecting the gel coat with a good wax coating or other UV protectants. The newer nano-polymer coating, such as SK Easy Shine, provides UV protection and are easier to apply than traditional wax.

Routine Maintenance

Your various owner's manuals are the authority on what to service and the appropriate service intervals. What I provide here is a quick reference on those items to keep you safe and to protect your investment. Other periodic service items for motorhomes, such as engine and transmission service, are addressed in the chassis owner's manual.

1. **Tire Inspection**. See Section III, Tires and Batteries
2. **Tire Rotation**. I don't rotate trailer tires unless uneven wear is noted. Motorhomes should rotate tires as recommend by the chassis manufacturer.
3. **Wheel Bearing**. Newer production trailers may have Dexter Nev-R-Lube™ bearing requiring an annual inspection for wear. Other trailers should have the wheel bearings inspected and repacked every 12-24 months depending on actual milage.
4. **Break Inspection**. Same schedule as wheel bearings.
5. **Roof Seals and Caulking**. Inspect annually and repair/replace seals and caulk, as necessary. Units kept in covered storage may require less frequent inspections.

6. **Hot Water Heater**. Flush annually with fresh water. Replace nylon plug, as necessary. For Suburban (not Atwood) models you may have an Anode Rod which requires replacement every 18-24 months.
7. **Running Lights**. Check the brake, turn signal and marker lights each day before travel.
8. **Battery Fluid Level**. Check the flooded lead acid battery fluid level every 45 to 60 days. Add water when needed and use only *distilled water*. All other battery types should not require periodic maintenance.
9. **Weight Distribution Hitch**. Check for excessive wear, rust or damage each time you hitch the trailer. Apply a thin coat of lithium grease to the hitch ball and clean the inside of the hitch coupler with a dry cloth.
10. **LP System Leaks**. If a smell of LP is present the system needs to be checked for leaks. Use a spray bottle of soapy water to spray on fittings and connections looking for bubbles. Replace leaking hoses and fittings or seek professional assistance.

Notes:

Campground Etiquette

Campgrounds have written and posted rules mostly to protect the property, mitigate liability issues, pet control and to comply with local laws and ordinances. On the other hand, the camping community at large has unwritten rules known as campground etiquette that help to promote harmony among the campers and to set the boundaries of what is considered good behavior when explicit rules are not available.

Being a good neighbor and considerate of others pretty much covers everything and should suffice by itself. Sometimes a Newbie doesn't yet understand the ropes so we can help them learn and maybe make a new friend along the way. But unfortunately, there is a small yet growing number of people that do not know what being a good neighbor really means. I'm quite sure you do not fall into this group since you were kind enough to purchase my book, but I wanted to make a list of "best practices" you can show to others when they misbehave.

1. Wave and say hello to other campers, you don't have to stop what you are doing and hold a long conversation but just recognize them as fellow campers.

2. Give campers a chance to completely setup or break camp before engaging in conversation. Most have a routine or checklist to follow and we don't want to be a distraction.

3. Do not walk across someone's campsite or use it as a shortcut. Respect their space as if they own the property and you own your property (campsite).

4. Don't burn trash, cardboard, or plastic in the fire pit, it smokes and smells. Smoke cannot be avoided and is expected but keep it natural.

5. Leave the campsite cleaner than you found it. All trash, cigarettes butts, bottle tops should be placed in the trash bin. Do not throw or leave trash in the fire pit for others to deal with.

6. The campsite has an authorized max number of people, don't hold a large family reunion or party without management approval. Even with approval be considerate to other campers.

7. Loud music is never an option. If you must have outside music or television keep the volume reasonable for your immediate campsite only. Other campers will select their own music.

8. Keep bikes, toys, and other obstacles out of the street, it is hard enough navigating a large RV on small access lanes so keep it clear and others will appreciate your effort. This also goes for parking in general and especially for boats, 4-wheelers, and tow vehicles.

9. Follow the campground rules for pets. Don't let dogs bark, keep them on a leash and pickup their poop. Even if your pet is well behaved or trained, this doesn't give you the right to not use a leash.

10. Children should not wonder off and play on other campsites without permission. Hopefully, the campground will provide a safe place other than the street for children to play but if they don't ensure you monitor children closely for everyone's safety.

11. Outside lights are usually permitted but with consideration to others. Bright lights left on overnight can and will shine into nearby campsites and may present a problem sleeping for some. Besides, it is great to see some stars when camping so keep the lights to a minimum.

12. Quiet hours are usually defined by campground management and must be observed. This means the party is over, move inside if you must and allow others to go to bed quietly. Generators are prohibited during quiet hours just as is any other noise making

device left outside. You can run air conditioners since they are considered essential.

13. Don't arrive late or depart early. Respect the quiet hours and try to arrive at the campground before quite hours begin. Likewise, if departing in the early hours of the morning try to complete as much of the outside preparation as you can the night before.

14. Respect the environment. Don't leave food on the ground, keep your trash organized and disposed of properly, do not dump wastewater on the ground and if you do smoke be conscience of where your smoke is drifting and how close your neighbors are.

When or should you get campground management involved if people are "acting up" at the campground? The first question to ask, "If needed, is management even available after hours?" Most state and national campgrounds will have a camp host onsite and available 24/7. Other campgrounds without a camp host should have an emergency number listed on your receipt or other check-in documents.

For things like trash, pet droppings and cutting through a campsite I would just try to offer a friendly reminder of the correct way to do the activity. Sometimes a simple reminder can apply enough peer pressure to get the unacceptable activity corrected. And this also goes for loud music or running generators after hours as well. For repeat offenders or if you know you will be facing resistance go directly to the camp host. We are campers looking for fun and adventure, confrontation is not what we signed up for.

Some of the worst problems found at a campground are the unreported problems for which the campground management should take for action and correct. If the campground is dirty, unkept and rules are generally not followed the campground will only get worse as times passes. It doesn't hurt to make a few suggestions to the host upon departing. Who knows, something may change for the better.

Campers are friendly people, and we all have the opportunity and obligation to carry on this tradition. We help others when needed, share our tools and knowledge when asked and enjoy a warm campfire with neighbors at the end of the day. We are all in this together so follow campground etiquette and I'll remind you to unhook the water hose and pick up your chocks before driving off. I'm sure I would tell you anyway even if your neighboring skills were somewhat lacking.

Notes:

Top Ten Items for a New RV

In the old days it was customary for the selling dealer to provide a complementary package of RV essentials to get you started. In today's world you are lucky to get a tank of propane, fuel in the motorhome tank and a packet of sewer treatment chemicals. And this is because the dealer has a showroom RV store where you can purchase these things providing you have any money left after paying for the RV.

Be smart and a little cheap when it comes to outfitting your new RV and do this before you take delivery. Walmart is less expensive than the RV store but extremely limited in selection. The hardware store and home improvement stores are good for plumbing and electrical items. Just be careful that the items you purchase will function in an RV.

If you don't yet shop and purchase products online, I encourage you to take the plunge and start saving money instantly. Amazon can be your best friend knowing there is a surge of things you will need for that first camping experience, but it won't end there. As you camp more and interact with other campers you will discover an unlimited number of "things" that can make camping better, smarter, more convenient, safer, and not to mention more automated.

To get you started I'm not only going to name the products but I'm providing specific recommendations and that is for a reason. I want you to be successful as quickly as possible and not take several years to learn which black tank treatment prevents odors and not merely covers them up. Or to allow you the unpleasant experience of learning that cheap sewer hoses always fail while you are dumping the black tank therefore creating a huge mess.

Top Ten Items

1. Happy Campers Organic RV Holding Tank Treatment
2. Camco RhinoFLEX 20' RV Sewer Hose Kit
3. Drinking Water Hose - 25' Premium Lead-Free

4. Taste Pure RV/Marine Filter with Flexible Hose Protector
5. Tire Covers set of 4, Measure to Fit
6. Wheel Chocks - Solid Rubber Heavy Duty
7. Jack Pads/Leveling Blocks
8. Patio Carpet/Cover - 9 x 12 Reversible
9. Electrical 50-to-30-amp Adapter or Electrical 30-to-50-amp Adapter
10. Progressive Industries EMS Portable RV Surge Protector (30 or 50-Amp)

Pro Tip: Get nothing unless you know why you need it and how to use it. The Internet is full of recommendations for new RV owners and that is fine but don't go blindly into the RV store. The list above is prepared to keep you out of trouble knowing that all the comfort items will come later.

An RV is much like a puppy you must feed it frequently, give it lots of naps and in return you get unlimited joy and love. This short list of essentials is just an appetizer to hold you over until the main course. Take your time in outfitting your RV and learn as you go. What works for your neighbor is good to know but what works for you is yet to be known.

Notes:

Generator or Solar?

One of my favorite subjects is alternative power sources. I have configured and installed several solar systems; workshop, carport, chicken coop, and of course I have the factory solar on my travel trailer. There is something about snagging some "free" electricity that I think intrigues us all.

For generators, I seem to have a small collection and currently I'm down to only three. It is almost a necessity to have a backup generator living in a hurricane zone like I do. But for some reason I just enjoy maintaining my generators and I get a lot of satisfaction when they are put to work during a power outage.

Off-grid camping is becoming more popular and is one of the "justifications" we have in owning a travel trailer. With our travel trailer configured with solar and a generator we can be spontaneous, agile, and ready to setup camp almost anywhere. I think a lot of you have some boondocking or dry camping in your future but may be unsure or confused about the electrical power situation when camping without shore power. A little planning and preparation now will go a long way to saving some sleepless, cold nights and maybe a few dead batteries.

Before we get into the details, take pen and paper and list the electrical appliances and devices you expect to operate when boondocking. Don't forget things like the water pump, furnace (blower motor) and a charging capability for your cellphones and laptops. This will help in understanding your power needs and determine if you need solar or a generator or both.

Solar Power

To best understand solar sometimes it is easier to understand what solar "is not." We can do this by resolving some of the common myths about solar power.

- Solar is cheap
- Solar can run anything
- Solar can be used anywhere
- Solar is hard or complex to maintain

There are calculations on the cost of solar such as a 2017 study stating that by 2020 solar power will cost $0.06 per kilowatt-hour. This is way more complex than what we need to discuss here, and these types of figures are always geared to larger installations such as homes or businesses. For us RVers, the question becomes, "What is the cost of keeping my batteries charged and preventing premature battery failure?" We also need to consider that the solar cost includes not only solar panels but also a charge controller, battery bank, monitoring devices, associated wiring, and labor charges. The only way you will fully recoup the expense of solar in your RV is through the comfort and pleasure solar brings to your camping experience and it won't take very long to realize the true benefits of solar.

A solar power system is nothing more than a battery charger. When thinking about what solar power can operate, think in terms of, "What can my batteries operate." You will realize that high amperage devices like air conditioning, microwave ovens, hot water heaters, space heaters and hair dryers will quickly or immediately drain most battery banks. Solar is great for maintaining the battery for operation of all 12v DC devices like lights, fans, furnace blowers and refrigerators. The Inverter can be used for small 110v AC needs such as televisions, entertainment systems and charging cellphones and laptops. *Refer to the Electrical Systems chapter to learn more about Inverters.*

To generate the amperage necessary for battery charging solar panels require clear, unobstructed exposure to the sun. This is referred to as harvesting power. Panels loose efficiency quickly with shade or other obstructions which reduce the amount of sunlight. Portable solar panels, such as a Solar Suitcase, can be positioned in direct sun exposure while your Airstream cools in the shade. A combination of both rooftop and portable panels is an optimal solution when boondocking.

Maintaining a solar system is almost like flying on autopilot. Other than monitoring the system to ensure it is performing as expected and cleaning the solar panels periodically, there is nothing to do. Maintaining the batteries, especially if they are flooded lead acid type will require periodic maintenance which is addressed in other sections of this book.

Determining the appropriate size or amount of solar is really limited only by the number and size of the panels which will fit on the rooftop. The basic 180-watt system supplemented with a 100-watt solar suitcase (if necessary) will be sufficient for most everyone. Regardless of the solar capacity you choose, it should be sufficient to charge the battery bank. For example, if you are planning for multiple 100 amp-hour Lithium batteries, you will need more solar panels than a smaller configuration such as 2 80 amp-hour flooded lead acid batteries.

Pro Tip: Estimate the number of amp-hours you expect to use daily, then select the size and number of solar panels necessary to replace those amp-hours in the battery bank.
(amps x hours used = amp-hours) (watts used / volts = amps)

The bottom line on solar is to understand your needs and the limitations of solar. Solar is becoming standard equipment on more recreational vehicles, and I feel it should be standard on all, therefore I recommend if you have the opportunity for a solar upgrade get at least an entry level package.

Notes: Estimate your amp-hour usage. Simplified rough estimate. *Refer to the Appendix Q&A for typical appliance wattage usage.*

My daily watts: _____ (total watts from appliances & lights)

My daily amps: _____ (watts divided by volts = amps)

My daily amp-hours: _____ (amps multiplied by hours used)

Generators

For camping a generator is not needed; that is unless you want to keep your batteries charged and about a dozen other things when you don't have an electrical hookup. Let me explain.

Managing your resources is essential regarding water, electricity, and wastewater disposal. We have learned that solar is great, but it does have limitations and bridging these power limitations is where generator power comes in to play.

Generators are great for powering all the 110v AC devices which solar cannot accommodate such as air conditioning, microwaves, etc. Also, generators are essential in keeping the batteries charged when solar isn't enough such as on rainy days, limited sun exposure and when solar is just overwhelmed and cannot keep up with excessive power usage. When camping in warm weather, nothing cools like an air conditioner which can only be operated with shore power or a sufficiently sized generator.

A generator rated above 3000 watts is sufficient to operate typical RV air conditioners; one AC unit at a time. It will also operate a microwave oven, TV, and small kitchen appliances. Just remember to estimate your power consumption and don't exceed the generator's rating. Some campers use 2 smaller generators hooked together such as the Honda 2200 units. These smaller generators are lighter, coming in at around 40 pounds where the 3000-watt units start at about 95 pounds and go up from there.

Generators operate on either gasoline or liquid propane (LP) and in diesel motorhomes you may have a diesel generator. Many generators are fueled by gasoline and in comparison, to LP models, operate a little more efficiently since gasoline by volume produces higher BTUs. Each fuel type has pros and cons and over time I have come to prefer a Dual Fuel generator which will operator on either gasoline or LP. I rarely use gasoline in my generator; I just connect the generator to the onboard LP tanks and I'm good to go. I would not recommend transporting gasoline or a gasoline generator inside an RV, automobile or SUV.

Other than fuel type, wattage capacity and weight, the other major consideration is noise. Generator noise in the campground should be minimized as a courtesy to other campers. Therefore, is it a must to get an Inverter Generator. Inverter generators not only run with much less noise they also produce much "cleaner" pure sine wave power that is better and safer for sensitive electronics. The open frame "construction generators" are much cheaper, very heavy, and readily available. However, the noise level produced by these generators are not acceptable in typical camping locations but may be fine for remote camping without close by camping neighbors.

This is a comparison of some of the popular inverter generator models available.

Model	Watts*	Plug**	Fuel	Lbs.	Price
Honda EU 2200	1800/2200	15a	Gas	47	$1100
Predator 2200	1600/2000	15a	Gas	47	$549
Honda EU3000	2800/3000	30a Gen Locking	Gas	155	$2200
Champion 3400 Dual Fuel	3100/3400	RV 30a	Gas/LP	95	$985
Predator 3500	3000/3500	30a Gen Locking	Gas	134	$899

* Rated Running Watts/Surge (Starting) Watts
** Locking Plug requires 30-amp adapter for Airstream connection

Even when setup at a campground with utilities, you never know when the campground's power will go out. It has happened to me several times. This is when you can hear the muffled sound of generators throughout the campground, knowing those lucky campers still have air conditioning, heating and of course a fully charged battery.

The following scenarios describing camping styles may help in determining when solar or generator power will be most beneficial.

Scenario 1 - LITTLE OR NO SOLAR & NO GENERATOR
Always camping with an electrical connection at the campsite. Storage site has an electrical connection to keep the battery charged.

Scenario 2 - MINIMUM OR MODERATE SOLAR
Usually camping with an electrical connection at the campsite. Storage site does not have an electrical connection but has available sun exposure for solar to maintain the battery charge. Limited boondocking may be possible.

Scenario 3 - MODERATE SOLAR & GENERATOR
Occasional boondocking or dry camping for just a few days at a time depending on available generator fuel.

Scenario 4 - LARGE SCALE SOLAR & GENERATOR
Frequent boondocking or dry camping for extended periods of time.

Just remember that any boondocking or dry camping scenario with anticipated high amperage device usage will require a generator with sufficient capacity. Generator fuel consumption can be expensive. Maximize your solar power capability and view the generator as a backup power source to replenish the battery and supplement the solar as needed.

Pro Tip: When boondocking, charging the battery once in the morning and again just before bedtime should keep everything in check, battery wise, just monitor your power consumption.

Notes:

Jack Hunnicutt

Part VII

Sometimes you just need an adventure to cleanse the bitter taste of life from your soul.

~Unknown

Devil's Tower - Wyoming

Are We There Yet?

When asked "Are we there yet?" I always like to say, "We have never been closer." Wish I could say a few words here to remove any of your remaining anxieties, stress and just plan worry but all of that will subside with experience. There are just a few more remaining areas to address, so we are not quite "there" yet.

You have seen me using words and phrases like *proactive, mindset, your process, and ready to drive*. When I do, I'm speaking to you as an individual since each reader will eventually develop "their own way" and that is expected. The notes you have collected are what makes this a unique learning experience. Each reader will walk away with a different knowledgebase specifically designed for their situation and their RV.

If you haven't noticed yet, this book has been all about managing outcomes, avoiding unwanted surprises, and getting the most out of your RVing experience. Here in Part VII, we complete the picture by talking about your pets, setting expectations for service and maintenance, then taking a peeking into what the future may hold.

Get ready to pull it all together, you have the individual pieces of knowledge and now you only need the ribbon and bow to complete the package.

Pets are Campers Too

From my causal observations I would say thirty to fifty percent of RV owners travel with pets. And there are many different types of pets, but I will focus here on cats and dogs since they are most common and the most welcomed at campgrounds.

Each campground will have rules addressing pets which can vary significantly from campground to campground. Never assume your pets will be permitted in the campground until you have read the specific rules and guidance. If you have unique pets or considerations call ahead and verify your pets are welcome. If you don't agree with the campground's policy on pets don't try to bend the rules, simply find a different place to camp.

Some campgrounds have specific rules addressing the so-called exotics such as lizards, snakes, monkeys, and other critters not considered domestic animals. Always ask first.

Before You Go

Pets have their own mind regardless of how well trained they may be. Wondering away from the campsite always leads to trouble with either a neighbor or getting lost. It does happen and nothing is sadder than a camper having to leave their pet behind because it wondered off.

Please have you pet microchipped and use a collar that has your contact information embossed or attached. Your Vet can help with the microchip and get you pet registered with a nationwide pet locator service. Pet collars with a name and phone number are available for less than fifteen dollars. These two items working together **are the only way** to ever get your pet back if lost.

Out of the hundreds of campgrounds we have visited only one has required proof of rabies vaccination. We carry a copy of their vaccinations in the glovebox with the vehicle registration and insurance cards. It your travels take you across the Canadian or Mexican borders

124

you will require more documentation. I'm not listing specific border crossing requirements here since they may and do change. Check the Internet for the most current information.

Of course, you want to know exactly where the pets will ride when traveling. Pack the necessary food, toys, bedding and do not forget the leash. The leash is a must have any time your pet exits the tow vehicle or RV. Keeping them close at hand protects your pet and may protect other animals from being provoked if your pet gets too close. Even if your pet has been trained to walk off leash you should continue to use the leash to show others your pet is under control.

Cats are cool and always do their own thing and only once have I seen a camper allow their cat to walk freely around the campsite. Since everyone knows cats are usually better protected when indoors, most of the following narrative is about dogs.

Aggressive Breeds

I really hate this label and had rather change it to *aggressive humans* since dogs learn to be aggressive and are not born that way as part of their breed. Granted some breeds have an aggressive tendency but dogs are individuals and should be considered as such and not stereotyped. Unfortunately, some campgrounds have a list of breeds they consider aggressive and are excluded from entrance.

This is not limited to campgrounds, but insurance companies follow similar practices. Once when seeking homeowner's insurance, I admitted I had a German Shepherd Dog and the agent said he could not write the policy, then he said, "if you say he is a mixed breed and not full blood we won't have a problem." I understand the motive may be the campground's liability insurance exclusions for certain breeds. This doesn't make it right, but we must respect their position.

Staying Home Alone

Let's face it, you just can't take the pets everywhere you go especially when sightseeing and visiting major attractions. Leaving them in an unattended vehicle is never an option and illegal in many states especially in the South and Southwest where the high temperatures in a closed vehicle can **seriously injure or kill within minutes**.

Leaving pets "home alone" in the RV may be an option under most situations. Always consider the safety aspect first such as expected temperatures, sufficient water, toys and what happens should the electricity unexpectantly go out? Also consider your pets temperament and energy level. You don't want to return finding holes chewed in the woodwork or cushions torn apart.

Campgrounds may have rules against leaving pets alone so check first. Dogs that bark when left alone will cause problems for your neighbors and should be avoided.

Pro Tip: Whether you leave pets alone or not, it is a good idea to post a sticker on the outside of the door stating you have pets inside and provide an emergency cell phone number in case of emergencies. You can also download a smartphone app to locate the nearest Veterinary Clinic in case of an emergency.

Notes:

RV Defects are Normal

It is with openness and honesty that I write this chapter therefore leaving what some may perceive to be the bad news coming at the end of the book. It is always better to manage our expectations than to "stress over seeking perfection when just good enough will do." This is a sloppy quote of an excellent concept, but I think you get the picture.

Looking at the RV Industry as a whole, RV defects are normal or so it seems from the perspective of the manufacturer and selling dealerships. If not, then why is it so common for some new owners to spend the first few months "working out the bugs?" Or in many instances, the owners themselves perform the repairs to avoid long waiting times at the service repair shop and to ensure the job is done right the first time.

Almost every high-ticket product we purchase today touts their quality, craftsmanship or product longevity except recreational vehicles for the most part. Just look at any automobile commercial which is chock full of references to how well they are built, detailing the over-the-top comfort level and quality of materials. You also see pretty much the same gloating for typical household appliances like refrigerators and washing machines. Some RV manufactures try to do this same thing, but their track record is difficult to cover up.

How do I know all this? In addition to owning RVs for almost 20 years I recently conducted Internet polling to learn how RV Owners felt about the quality of their RV. The results were no surprise, or at least not to me a retired process and quality engineer. But understand there are many owners across the country that are incredibly happy with their unit which isn't quite enough for me. I believe every RV owner should be a Happy Campers.

First some numbers to study to understand the focus and target groups involved with the polling next we will look at the specific Grades owners have assigned to their RV.

I conducted two polls, one for Airstream owners and the second for all other RV brand owners. Asking these same questions, you will see in the following graphic to both groups.

Participants were asked to select the statement that best describes their opinions about the quality of their 2018-2021 model year RV. There were 238 Airstream respondents, 313 for all other RV brands respondents totaling 551 responses.

I view these polls much like an election exit poll, they do show trends however accuracy increases as the size of the sampled group increases. For fairness three caveats should be considered.

1) The poll was made available to over 200K RV owners as members of Facebook Groups
2) Negative remarks are more freely shared on the Internet than positive experiences, just a fact of human nature
3) Online polls were available for a period of 3 days

Which Statement Best Describes Your RV Quality	
A+	No Issues to Report
A	Minor Issues 1 Service Visit
B	Minor Issues More Than 1 Service Visit
C	Major issues More Than 1 Service Visit
D	Major Issue Cancelled Trip
F	One Problem After the Other - Still Broke

As a sign of what was to come, the first two comments were owners asking why I had not included a "No Issues to Report" category? I immediately added the category and was surprised at how many respondents selected "No Issues to Report."

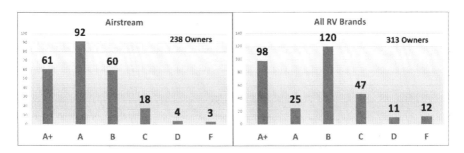

From this set of graphics nothing really jumps out and gives quality a thumbs up or down. One indicator may be the D and F grades for All RV Brands or the 92 (37%) Airstream Owners selecting Grade A and 98 (31%) All RV Brand Owners feeling Grade A+ is their best fit.

Not convinced one way or the other yet? I'm not either so let's do a deeper dive and ask the numbers to present a different picture.

In these next charts I combined the top two grades (A+ and A) and the bottom two grades (D and F) which should represent the most satisfied and most dissatisfied customers for each group.

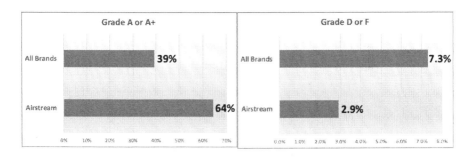

The picture comes in much better focus from this perspective, at least for me. Over 60 percent of Airstream Owners assigned Grade A or A+ showing their level of satisfaction, however 2.3 percent of Airstream Owners had to "cancel trips because of major issues" or "experiencing one issues after the other and it is still broke."

129

The All-Other Brands group reported quite a different situation. Only 39 percent of these owners are assigning Grade A or A+ and the owners living with the D or F grades is 7.3 percent of the All-Other Brands group.

Where do all these defects come from and why? The price of anything is a factor of materials and the cost of doing business, simplified of course. Manufacturers, to control expenses, have chosen production practices based on a timeline consistent with getting products to customers as quickly as possible. Dealerships gladly accept products with "sure to find" defects which provide a steady flow of warranty repair work keeping their service departments fully engaged although usually not fully staffed. The maintenance waiting game begins here.

The cost of quality must fall on someone's plate, the question becomes who and when? The reality is that if there is any quality at all to be had it is the buyer who absorbs the expense of quality knowingly or not and will be better off for it. We don't see Quality as a line item on the invoice nor can we tell the manufacturer "Hold the Quality" on this one to reduce the price. It is what it is.

Seeing the big picture from both the manufacture's and buyer's perspectives I think we can see that the process although troublesome is working. The manufactures ship products and the buyers find an affordable deal. The long and short of the RV Industry is that RV defects are normal.

This is not really bad news at all. I used this chapter to pull together much of what we have already learned. Knowing and understanding all the systems and components help significantly in dealing with these so-called defects or problem issues. Many things we can fix ourselves and we should. As previously noted why endure a long wait to get your RV back from some minor repairs? If you go into RV ownership blindly you will be at the mercy of repair shops for everything causing much stress and it will be expensive.

I will point you back to the chapter on Taking Delivery and conducting the Pre-Delivery Inspection. This is exactly where you can get an understanding of the level of quality that went into building your RV and take some action to enhance the quality immediately.

If recreational vehicles were delivered in perfect condition with the best materials possible and a guarantee of zero failures for the life of the warranty, we would not be able to afford that RV. I'm not saying to go quietly into the night and just accept what you get, but I am saying try to be satisfied with this whole complex system of the RV Industry but hold everyone accountable.

> **Pro Tip**: You really do get what you pay for. Don't go cheap on tires and batteries and understand that lower end RV brands will have more below par materials than higher end brands. Regardless, of entry level or luxury, all units will have issues. Having a good maintenance relationship will make your overall RV experience more enjoyable.

Notes:

Subjects Left Out

As a reader myself, when I finish a book I like to reflect on what I just read and do a little critique on what I liked and how I might have done things differently. One thing I don't like is gaps or missing information in a story. With a "how to" or "do it yourself" book like *My RV Mentor*, rarely can a complex subject like this address every nuance and characteristic. I hope I have covered everything necessary to make you a successful RV owner however some omissions were intentional.

One reason for omissions, as you will learn in the next few pages, is for this book to provide value to the reader for years to come and not to focus on transitory technologies and subjects that will become irrelevant or outdated in the short run. The other "non-focus" subjects I don't address are the activities that happen in and around the RV such as cooking, indoor entertainment, decorating, and travel destinations.

However, with today's tidal wave of new owners and owners rethinking their RVing strategy, I would be remis not to mention the following areas if not to only acknowledge their importance.

Cost of Ownership

How much does all this cost? To tell you the truth I can't even estimate at a high level what your expenses will be because there are so many factors that go into determining actual cost. And if I did profile my expenses and later you realized something different, you may be very disappointed or may even have accumulated debt you had not planned for because of my examples.

In the first few pages of the book, I identified some RV owner's constraints where I generalized that, "for the average family, it can and probably will be expensive." I have identified many of the expenses over and beyond the initial expense of buying your RV without quantifying how much. I talked about shopping online to save money and not to buy anything recreational vehicle related unless you know why you are buying it, and how to use it one you get it. One example is a new owner purchasing a surge protector for several hundred dollars and letting it sit in the storage compartment because they knew it was important but didn't know how to use it. One example is a new owner purchasing a surge protector for several hundred dollars and letting it sit in the storage compartment because they knew it was important but didn't know how to use it or when to use it.

Just to make sure we cover as much as we can without having to dust off our crystal ball (estimates are impossible without established data), here are some typical expenses.

Annual Vehicle Registration: My tow vehicle registration is $95 in Florida. I know people in the West paying $1200 per year and up for a similar vehicle. Each state is different and what one state charges cannot be used to estimate cost in a different state.

Insurance: Motorhomes are insured much like an automobile but with possibly higher liability coverage. Trailers are usually insured in conjunction with the tow vehicle (not always). Some factors considered in determining cost of insurance include value of the RV, year, age of drivers and past driving history, credit score, state and city where the unit will be stored, and how frequently used. Rarely will two RV owners fall under the exact same insurance profile.

Maintenance: After warranty maintenance labor charges can vary from $95 to $195 per hour or more. Those of you that can do some of your own maintenance will reduce costs significantly. Just doing your own oil change could save fifty dollars or more. *Refer to the owner's manual to better understand type and frequency of routine maintenance.*

Camping Fees: The average camping fee can be anything from $20 to $140 per night depending on location and amenities. Generally, I try to avoid anything over $40 unless it is a destination campground. You will have to find your groove and set thresholds on nightly camping expenses. Each trip will require some planning to include anticipated expenses.

Fuel Expense: Fuel prices can jump up overnight due to severe weather or political climate at home or abroad. And the prices always come down much slower if they come down at all. State taxes have a huge impact on the final price of fuel making some states more expensive to visit than others. An RV salesman once told me, "If gasoline goes to $5/gallon I can't give away motorhomes." Again, fuel expenses should be part of your trip planning process.

Storage Fees: Many homeowner's associations, local laws and ordinances prohibit RV parking or storage in residential areas. Finding suitable, secure, and affordable storage can be a challenge. Of course, covered storage is preferred but can run $100 to $300 per month or more in some metropolitan areas. The cheapest bare lot parking I have seen is $45 per month which provides little to no security other than a fence. Storage fees are frequently forgotten or not realized until after the RV purchase.

Unexpected Expenses: We talked about tire and battery failure and I provided some tips on how to prevent premature failures. But the odds are, sooner or later you may have a blowout and your battery will only last so long then it will require replacement. Trip interruption expenses include hotels, meals and transportation costs should your RV require major repairs while on a trip. Should you have insurance to cover some of these unexpected expenses? Maybe, it depends on your specific situation.

Of course, I have not even mentioned, food, entertainment, entrance fees and all that stuff that tourist do. Knick knacks, a few refrigerator magnets and I think you get the picture. It all starts to add up quickly if not managed. But I'm confident all of you are onboard with these types of expenses but simply needed a summary of what expenses are involved with maintaining and operating your RV.

Full-Time Living

I really wish I had some measurable figures to provide the numbers of people opting for full-time RV living but I don't. In the middle of this mass exodus from brick-and-mortar homes to the open road happening in front of our very eyes, it is extremely difficult to make estimates. The COVID-19 social distancing concerns transitioned hundreds of thousands of employees from an in-person workplace to working from home (telecommuting). This along with distance or virtual learning for school children and college students has freed us to reimagine home and classroom to any location or structure we wish.

Will this trend last? Will post-COVID expectations return everyone to the old norms of work and education requiring physical attendance? I believe full-time RV living is more of a social or economic issue than a matter of recreational living. Some of you may not agree with this but I define full-time as "living in your RV for as much of the future as you can predict." I'm seeing references to, "full-time for the next 3 months" or "full-time until we see everything" and again these are extended vacations, a temporary lifestyle changes but at least for me, not a full-time commitment.

To address full-time living opens the scope to domicile, residency, taxes, mail delivery, banking, insurance, medical care, obtaining medications, family, finances all in addition to living in a space offering little privacy from other family members living with you. This is a huge amount of subject matter requiring an additional book or two.

Staying Connected (Cellphone & Internet)

Are we really addicted to technology and all our various devices or are they an essential part of normal life? Regardless of your position on this subject, most of us want to stay connected to keep in touch with friends, family and as we are seeing today, this includes staying connected with work and school.

Cellphone coverage across the country can be hit and miss once you leave the footprint of the Interstate Highway System. Cell towers are placed in urban areas and along the major highways and throughfares to accommodate the most highly used locations.

Cellular signals are close but not absolute "line of sight" meaning if the cell tower (cell) can see your phone then you should get good reception. Cellular signals are blocked or decreased by obstructions such as building, mountains, and dense forest. Once again, camping is all about location, location, location. The further we venture away from the asphalt jungle the less likely it is that we can make a cellphone call. In this case, signal boosters or extenders may improve service.

Does using a different cellular carrier really make a difference? I have used all the big three, AT&T, Verizon, T-Mobile, and I have found little difference. Technologies are changing and all carriers are promising more if not better coverage in the future. For this reason, I'm not making any specific recommendations. Look for the deals and perks which also change almost daily. Lastly, don't forget those other carriers who in many cases piggyback the same networks as the big three.

Wi-Fi is the wireless technology used to connect computers, tablets, smartphones, smart televisions, and other devices to the Internet. For campers there are two primary methods to access Wi-Fi; connect to the campground's network if provided or via a cellphone or specialty device providing hotspot capability. It is becoming more common for commercial establishments outside of the campground to provide free Wi-Fi hotspots.

Campgrounds offering Wi-Fi will place one or more Wi-Fi antennas in central locations for access. The signal is usually stronger the closer you are to the campground office or activity buildings where the antennas may be located. A Wi-Fi booster can provide a stronger signal. However, if the campground's network is busy or overloaded (which is usually the case) the booster will not improve your service.

For areas without Wi-Fi service, you may use a cellphone hotspot providing you have a strong cellular signal, and your cell plan provides sufficient data (Megabits of Bandwidth). Unlimited data plans are available which is nice to access the Internet without additional devices or add-on plans. One limitation is streaming video which can cause the phone to heat up, but I have been highly successful uploading YouTube videos using a cellphone hotspot. Additionally, unlimited data plans usually throttle back or slow down your connection after a specific threshold has been exceed, such as with my plan after 50 gigabytes of data.

There are numerous cell boosters and extenders available on the market today ranging in price from $25 to hundreds of dollars. Just as with cellular. technologies supporting wireless Internet are evolving. Therefore, again I do not have a specific recommendation other than to interact with fellow campers in person and on the Internet to learn about what is working best today.

CAUTION

No public or free Wi-Fi network is totally secure. You need to protect yourself and never do banking over a public or free Wi-Fi network. This warning applies to public or free Wi-Fi at airports, bus stations, coffee shops and campgrounds.

Renting Out My RV

More and more frequently I receive the question, "Can I rent my RV to help recover some of the cost?" My usual answer to the question is, "No, because your RV will never come back in the same condition as when it left, and you will have many regrets afterwards." But you may feel completely different on the subject and who knows, I could be completely wrong? I spell DEPRECIATION with Capital letters, how about you?

To hit the highlights of what I don't cover on this subject is; insurance, especially everything concerning liability, contracts and other legal issues, taxes, marketing, check in/check out, and the major issues of cleaning and repairs. By the way, how are you going to train the renter to operate all of the RV systems we have covered in this book in just a few minutes or maybe in an hour or two? It will be the blind leading the blind as the renter uses your beautiful RV to OJT their way into a rolling vacation.

Notes:

RV Newbie to Pro

Congratulations! It has been a pleasure to be your mentor knowing that you now have the necessary knowledge and skills to hit the road and enjoy your next adventure. We have come a long way together from making that first decision to buy an RV, walking through the buying process, understanding, and operating the various systems, planning a trip, enjoying the journey, and living the camper's life at the campground.

But I'm not going to completely turn you lose quite yet without planning and anticipating things that go bump in the night. Things will break, occasionally wear out, or sometimes just become stubborn. This is where the following Q&A an Troubleshooting Guide comes into action to help sort out the issues and to offer solutions or in some cases recommend professional assistance. Bookmark these pages for quick and easy access because when you need this guidance you will be stressed (hopefully not too much), possibly frustrated and always in a rush. It is not the end of the world; you have training and now you are a Professional RV Owner. You and I together will get everything fixed and get back on the road to being happy campers again.

At your leisure I strongly encourage you to explore all the resources I have compiled for you. At the time of writing this book I have produced over 60 RV related videos available to you on my YouTube Channel with more being added monthly. For real-time information join the Facebook Group "My RV Mentor" to receive quick answers and advice from hundreds of fellow RV owners. In depth information and behind the video scenes are available on my Blog.

One great way to retain your knowledge is to share it with others. Take on mentoring someone or just be prepared to help when you see a fellow camper struggling at the campground. It's amazing how someone's problem can stimulate your learning and suddenly their problem expands your experience and becomes part of your lasting knowledge.

Take the Challenge

To demonstrate your knowledge, I encourage you to take my challenge and complete all these milestones in the first year of ownership.

- Drive through a major city; on the Interstate will be fine.
- Ask for a back in campsite even when pull throughs are available.
- Dry Camp at least one night; consider a Walmart, Cracker Barrel, BLM or your driveway
- Camp at a National Park or Corps of Engineers Park (COE)
- Camp at a State Park or a membership club like Harvest Host
- Find a campground on your smartphone app and book a night
- Camp one night using the furnace
- Review at least one campground online

Looking to the Future

As it has been for the last many generations technology is advancing at a staggering rate. Sometimes I feel we have too much technology in recreational vehicles and I long for the simple light switch and televisions with only an On, Off and Channel button. But those days are gone, and although we may not be better for it, we must be smarter at what we do if not only to survive but to understand the environment in which we live. Learning never stops.

The RV you own today is probably not the RV you will own in 5 years. Your family structure may change, your needs and requirements may change, your financial situation may allow more comforts to creep into your lifestyle. Sadly, but true a small number of you will decide your life no longer has room for an RV. My message here is please don't discard this book, you may revisit some of these chapters while learning you next RV. And for this reason, I have attempted to keep this book timeless in nature in hopes the content may remain relative for years to come.

Hope to see you down the road.

Appendix

Jack Hunnicutt

Q&A

Troubleshooting Guide

Tools for Travel and Campsite

Resources

RV Jargon

Q & A

Q: How can I determine if my RV is 30 amp or 50-amp electrical service?

A: A power cord with 3 prongs is 30 amp and 4 prongs is 50-amp service.

Q: When connected to 30-amp shore power, can the air conditioner and microwave be operated at the same time?

A: Maybe not. It depends on what else is currently in operation, TV, converter, hair dryer, etc. Use this chart to approximate power consumption.

Device or Appliance	Watts	Amps
Air Conditioner 15,000 BTU	1300-1800 Running	12-16
Refrigerator 12V	24-48 Running	2 - 4
Furnace 30,000 BTU	96	8
Lights - LED - Each	5 - 10	.4 - .8
Hair Dryer	1500	14
Microwave Oven	1100	9
Television	50	.5
Space Heater	800-1400	7 - 13
Residential Refrigerator	150 Running	1.5

Q: Why do the lights and fans have electrical power, but the microwave and air conditioner do not?

A: Remember the 2 electrical systems DC and AC? Without shore power the 110v devices like a microwave and air conditioner will not operate but the battery continues to supply the 12v devices such as lights and fans.

Q: What size generator is necessary to operate my RV?

A: It would require a huge and probably very loud generator to operate everything all at once. If the goal is to operate one air conditioner, keep the battery charged and maybe run the microwave then a 3300 watt or larger generator would do the job. Use the chart above to determine amp/watt usage.

Q: How long will a 30 lb. propane tanks last?
A: A 30 lb. propane tank has a 649,980 BTU capacity. As a rough comparison, a typical RV furnace will produce 30,000 BTU per hour. In this example one tank will last approximately 43 hours. Cooking and operating the refrigerator requires only a small amount in comparison.

Q: What causes sewer odor inside the RV?
A: Four common causes are: (1) Toilet seal allows sewer gas to enter the bathroom. Ensure the toilet can always hold a little water in the bowl. (2) Exhaust fan pulls sewer gas up from the black tank; do not run fan while flushing. (3) Ceiling fans pulling sewer gas off the roof from the tank vents. (4) Under sink pipe vent malfunction.

Q: Why is dirty water backing up in the shower drain?
A: This is an indication of gray tank overflow. Dump the gray tank water before putting any more water into the tank.

Q: What air pressure should be maintained in RV tires?
A: Each tire manufacturer has a tire inflation chart for each specific tire brand/model. Use the chart along with the actual RV weight to determine the correct air pressure.

Q: Can the awning be left extended at night or when away from the campsite?
A: It only takes a short burst of strong wind to damage the awning. My recommendation is to retract the awning every time you leave the RV and when you are not physically present and observing the awning such as at bedtime.

Q: Can the stabilizers be used to level the trailer?
A: Stabilizers are designed to reduce some of the motion in the trailer and not to support the weight of the trailer. Complete the leveling process before lowering the stabilizers.

Q: Slide outs will not retract; how can the RV be driven to a repair shop?

A: All slides (and jacks) have a manual mechanism. Usually, a socket and ratchet is used to manually retract the slide. Review the owner's manual for specific instructions.

Q: The RV is in storage without electrical shore power, will the batteries be okay?

A: Batteries must be stored fully charged meaning they require to be kept on the RV's converter with shore power, on a solar charging system or removed from the RV and placed on a multi-staged smart battery charger.

Q: How long can the RV sit without shore power before the batteries drain?

A: Each RV will be a little different based on the hidden or rogue battery drains. Generally, rule a fully charged battery should be fine for 5 to 10 days. Even with the battery disconnect switch engaged the RV will have a small battery drain.

Q: Water and moisture collect on the windows; how can this be controlled?

A: The moisture can be caused by cooking, taking showers and normal human and pet breathing. A small dehumidifier will remove the moisture while camping and it is also a superb way to keep humidity under control during periods of storage.

Q: What causes the smell of sulfur or rotten eggs?

A: Usually it is one of two causes. The hot water heater needs to be flushed to wash out minerals that can create an odor or lead acid batteries have boiled off fluid and the plates have become exposed.

Q: The weight distribution hitch makes noise when turning, is this normal?

A: Noise is normal which is caused by the friction of the WD bars on the retaining brackets. A small amount of lithium grease can be applied to the hitch ball.

Q: Can a passenger or pet ride in the trailer when towing?

A: In most and probably all states it is illegal for a passenger to ride in the trailer. Additionally, it is not a good idea to place a pet under those conditions either. When in motion it is very noisy in the trailer and the movement is much more pronounced than what is experienced in the tow vehicle. Typically, items are tossed around when traveling so clearly passengers and pets do not need that experience.

Q: How long do tires and batteries last?

A: Regardless of condition or appearance RV tires should be replaced every 4 to 6 years and sooner if the tires begin to show cracking, sidewall damage or any bulges or tread separation. Lead acid batteries if properly maintained should last 4 to 6 years. Lithium batteries may have a service life up to 10 years or possibly longer.

Q: Are older recreational vehicles denied at some campgrounds?

A: Sadly, the answer is yes but the good news is this is rarely considered at most campgrounds. Older campers will never have a problem making reservations at State and National Parks.

Q: Why do Class A motorhomes not come with a spare tire?

A: The tires are large between 19.5" and 22.5" diameter and are difficult to store. In case of a tire failure, the roadside service will either have to repair the tire or obtain a new tire.

Q: Can I walk on the roof of my RV?

A: It depends on the specific RV. For motorhomes and fifth wheels the answer is usually yes, however, for some travel trailers such as Airstream you can only stand or specific supported areas of the roof.

Q: Where can propane tanks be refilled?

A: Most truck stops such as Flying J and Pilot have facilities to refill both removable tanks and fixed tanks on a motorhome. U-Haul rental locations usually have propane refill capabilities.

Q: When purchasing an RV should a professional inspector be used to verify the condition of the RV?

A: Usually not when buying a new RV. Just follow a good process for conducting the pre-delivery inspection. I recommend contracting a professional inspector when purchasing a pre-owned RV such as the National RV Inspectors Association nrvia.org.

Q: Should I use the toilet and holding tank for "everything," or should I go to the bathhouse to do my "business?"

A: Of course, use the toilet. The toilet and holding tank are designed for all human waste making the RV fully contained unit. And yes, you can flush toilet paper; use adequate water and proper paper. *Refer to the RV Holding Tank chapter for specifics on paper and tank chemical treatments.*

Troubleshooting Guide

Problem: I have shore power and the microwave works but the electrical outlets don't.

Common Cause: GFCI breaker has tripped.

Solution: Find the outlet/breaker that controls the GFCI outlets and reset. The GFCI reset is usually in the bathroom but it could be in the kitchen. On some RVs I have seen the GFCI inside the breaker panel.

Problem: I'm on a 30-amp system and the breakers keep tripping.

Common Cause: Circuit overload. Too many electrical devices operating at the same time.

Solution: On 30-amps it is difficult to run anything in addition to one air conditioner and maybe a TV. The big amperage devices are electric hot water heater, air conditioner and microwave oven. Any two of these will usually trip breakers. When you start to add an electric space heater, coffee maker and hair dryers you will have to manage their use closely.

Problem: My lights and fans work but nothing else.

Common Cause: Loss of 110v or Shore Power.

Solution: Check the breaker on the campground power pedestal outside. If not working check the RV breaker box. A quick way to determine if you have shore power is look for the clock on the microwave oven even flashing mean you have 110v power.

148

Problem: My jacks, levelers and slides will not operate.

Common Cause: Weak battery or tripped breakers/fuses. These devices use a large amount of DC amperage and a weak battery may not provide enough current for them to operate.

Solution: Plug in to shore power and charge the battery or use jumper cables to jump the battery while operating the devices. It is a good practice to plug in to shore power when available before operating jacks, levelers, and slides. The shore power will top off the batteries and provide extra amperage boost.

Problem: Jacks, levelers or slides will not operate.

Common Cause: Tripped breaker or blown fuse. Frequently these devices will have inline fuses or micro-breakers on circuit control boards.

Solution: Reset breakers or replace fuses. Carry extra blade fuses and glass tube fuses.

Problem: When I connect to City Water my freshwater tank fills.

Common Cause: Water pump bypass valve clogged.

Solution: Clear the debris in the pump's bypass valve; this could be a small amount of sand preventing the valve from operating.

Problem: Water pressure in the kitchen, shower or bathroom sink is very low.

Common Cause: Blockage in the water line or faucet aerator.

Solution: Remove and clean aerator and check water filter for blockage. Check the campground freshwater connection for sufficient water flow. Recommend using a water pressure regulator set to 40-50 psi.

Problem: Air conditioner is dripping water on the inside of the RV.

Common Cause: Coils are frozen usually from low freon.

Solution: Turn off the air condition allowing the ice to melt then try operating it again. Schedule service appointment when available.

Problem: Lights or turn signals on the trailer do not work.

Common Cause: Loose or dirty connection on tow vehicle plug.

Solution: Secure plug and try again. If still not working, look inside plug using a flashlight and try removing and debris by blowing into the socket. You can use CRC Electrical Cleaner and Protectant if available.

Problem: Black tank or sewer odor inside RV.

Common Cause: Sewer gas coming up through toilet valve or ceiling vent fans pulling odor in from roof tank vent stacks.

Solution: Keep a small amount of water in the toilet bowl to prevent tank odor from coming into bathroom. Do not run the exhaust fan when flushing the toilet, this can draw sewer gas up from the tanks. And finally, check ceiling vents for pulling odor in from roof.

Problem: Smell of rotten eggs or sulfur inside RV

Common Cause: Mineral build up in hot water heater or exposed plates in battery.

Solution: Flush hot water heater tank. Remove the drain plug and rinse with fresh water using a wand type attachment on a water hose. If a battery is over-charged it may boil the water and sulfuric solution out of the battery and exposing the internal plates. The battery may become extremely hot and create a dangerous situation. Take precautions and use eye protect when checking the water level. The battery will require replacement.

Notes:

Tools for Travel and Campsite

Just like a Boy Scout, always be prepared especially when it comes to tools and other items to assist in making repairs. The nearest Walmart or Auto Zone can be hours away should you breakdown on a lonely West Texas highway or in some remote BLM camping area. This list of tools isn't to make a mechanic out of you but just enough to make some simple repairs or band aide fixes to get you back on the road.

Even with a good roadside assistance program you may still have to change a tire providing you have the right tools.

Tire Changing Tools
- Bottle Jack or if you have tandem axels you can use a RV tire changing ramp
- Lug nut wrench or breaker bar and correct size socket
- And of course, a good spare tire

General Tools
- Screwdriver set with a flat blade, Philips, and a small flat blade for tight spaces
- Set of small wrenches, 5/16, 1/4, 3/8, 7/16, 1/2 inch
- Pair of pliers, regular and needle nose
- Magnet on an extendable stick to reach small items like dropped screws
- Pair of scissors
- Razor blade knife

Other Handy Items
- Flashlight with extra batteries
- Electrical tape
- Duct tape
- Plumbers Teflon tape
- Silicon spray lube

- Extra leveling blocks
- Fuses, both blade fuses and glass tube fuses various sizes 3 to 15 amp
- Multimeter to check battery voltage
- Ant bait or spray

Pro Tips: A good Bit Driver Set offers more flexibility than a screwdriver set. Soak cotton balls in a mixture of equal parts borax, sugar and water then place around inside and outside to prevent and kill ants and roaches. And a headlamp (flashlight head strap) leaves both hands available to do the work.

Tools can be heavy, hard to keep organized, and difficult to store. And doesn't it seem like every time you go looking for a specific tool it is always in the last place you look. Sad attempt at humor but absolutely true. It may be more important to stay organized that it is to carry every tool for every situation. There is no need to go overboard because you can always borrow from others at the campground or dash down to Walmart. Use your money and storage space for those tools that may be necessary out on the highway where it can get awful lonely when you have a breakdown.

I tend to get boring when talking about tires and tire safety, but I find it difficult to apologize because I know you will thank me later. As previously discussed, tire failure is much more common than it should be and can quickly spoil a trip. Therefore, I do carry an air compressor to top off the tires when needed and to keep a trouble prone tire going until I can find a tire shop. The expense of keeping an air compressor onboard is not the problem it usually becomes an issue with storage space. For this reason (and because they perform so perfectly) I recommend the VIAIR Corporation series of compressors which are compact and come with a handy carry bag.

Notes:

Resources

These are resources I have developed and maintained to help fellow RV owners. Now my hope is for these resources to complement this book by building a broad yet concise set of learning media.

YouTube Channel

https://wwwyoutube.com/c/landingzonehome
Search on YouTube: LandingZoneHome
Many of my videos are focused directly on specific chapters of the book. For example, I have videos on Storage, Security, Safety, Holding Tanks, Fresh Water Cross-contamination, Boondocking and numerous videos on Campground Reviews. I also cover topics on Solar and Generator backup power.

Facebook Group

https://www.facebook.com/groups/myrvmentor
Search on Facebook: My RV Mentor
The Facebook Group, My RV Mentor, helps the new RV owner and anyone seeking assistance with the operation of their RV, planning a trip, camping, or on the road. What makes MY RV Mentor different is the opportunity to ask for one on one mentoring from an experienced RV owner willing to share their knowledge and offer advice. We have all been a Newbie at one time or another, so no question is "dumb" and the only bad question is the one you didn't ask

Blog

https://landingzonehome.blogspot.com/
Search on Google: Landing Zone Home Blog or click the link on my YouTube Channel
This is my latest effort at RV information sharing. On the Blog I periodically post topics on RV maintenance and upkeep and product reviews.

RV Jargon

5er – Fifth Wheel Trailer or Gooseneck

A
AC – Air Conditioner
AC – Alternating Current

B
Blue Boy - Portable Wastewater Tank
Boondocking - Camping with No Hookup

C
City Water – Water Provided at Campsite Faucet
Converter - Transforms Alternating Current to Direct Current for Battery Charging
CG - Campground
Class A – Motorhome Built on a Strong Bus or Truck Chassis
Class B – Motorhome Built on a Standard Van
Class C – Motorhome Built on a Van Cabin Chassis and Extended Body Structure

D
DC – Direct Current
Dog Bone - Electrical Adapter Allowing Use of 30-amp or 50-Amp Service
Diesel Pusher (DP) - Motorhome with Rear Diesel Engine
Dry Camping - Camping with No Hookups
Dump Station - Common Area with Facilities to Empty Holding Tanks

E
EPDM - Ethylene Propylene Diene Monomer Roof Material

F

Full-Time – Living in an RV as primary residence
FHU – Full Hookup
FRED - Motorhome with Front End Diesel Engine

G

GFCI - Ground Fault Circuit Interrupter
GVW - Gross Vehicle Weight
GVWR - Gross Vehicle Weight Rating
GCVWR - Gross Combined Vehicle Weight Rating

H

Hitch Coupler – Attaching Device for Hitch Ball to Trailer
HVAC – Heating and Air Conditioning
Hybrid Camper - Expandable Travel Trailer Sometimes with Soft Sides (Canvas)

I

Inverter - Produces Alternating Current from DC Battery Source

L

Low Point Drains - Valves to Completely Drain all Fresh Hot and Cold Water from RV
LP – Liquid Propane

M

MH – Motorhome

N

Non-Potable Water – Not for Human Consumption

P

Payload - The weight of passengers, liquids, pets, and cargo
PDI - Pre-Delivery Inspection
Popup Camper - Compact Collapsible or Folding Travel Trailer with Canvas Sides

156

Potable Water – Safe for Drinking, Bathing, Cooking
Pull Through - Campsite that has an Entrance and Exit without Backing Up

S
Seasonal – Living in an RV for a Specified Part of the Year
Self-Contained - RV with Bath, Toilet and Cooking Capabilities with Holding Tanks
Shore Power - Electrical Service Provided at Campsite
Slide Out – Room/Area Extension
Slider - Type of Fifth Wheel Hitch
Stinky Slinky - Sewer Hose
Surge Protector – Common Name for Device Preventing Electrical Damage to RV

T
Tiny Trailer - Small Travel Trailer
TOAD – Tow Behind Automobile aka Dinghy
Tow Dolly – Platform for Towing an Automobile
TPMS – Tire Pressure Monitoring System
TPO - Thermoplastic Polyolefin Synthetic Rubber Roof
Truck Camper - Camper that Sits in the Bed of a Pickup Truck
TT – Travel Trailer

W
WD – Weight Distribution (Hitch)
Winterize - Preparing an RV for Below Freezing Temperatures

Thank you for purchasing *My RV Mentor*. I sincerely hope it helps you to enjoy the adventure and to make the most of your RV camping experience. As you take your final notes, I ask that you please provide a book review on Amazon. This not only helps me as an author, but it also helps to inform our fellow RV Owners about this book and how it may help them.

Final Notes:

About the Author

Jack Hunnicutt is a life-long camping and recreational vehicle enthusiast who has owned motorhomes, travel trailers and fifth wheels. With his family and pets, he has traveled the United States coast to coast and border to border. He hits the road at every available opportunity and can be found anywhere from the Florida Keys to the Rocky Mountains. His favorite camping destinations are the Black Hills, Smokey Mountains and anywhere along the Gulf Coast.

His YouTube Channel has over 75 videos presenting the challenges and pleasures of the RV lifestyle with an emphasis on the New RV Owner. He has also created videos on solar electric and generator backup power. He has created and administered several Facebook Groups and a Blog. He resides in the Florida Panhandle with his wife and daughter.

Another book by the Author

My Airstream Mentor: How to "Airstream" For Beginners & the Well-Traveled

Made in the USA
Columbia, SC
30 January 2025

53017733R00098